THE SPECTRUM OF SOCIAL TIME

SYNTHESE LIBRARY

A SERIES OF MONOGRAPHS ON THE

RECENT DEVELOPMENT OF SYMBOLIC LOGIC

SIGNIFICS, SOCIOLOGY OF LANGUAGE,

SOCIOLOGY OF SCIENCE AND OF KNOWLEDGE

STATISTICS OF LANGUAGE

AND RELATED FIELDS

Editors:

B. H. KAZEMIER / D. VUYSJE

GEORGES GURVITCH

THE SPECTRUM OF
SOCIAL TIME

D. REIDEL PUBLISHING COMPANY / DORDRECHT-HOLLAND

La multiplicité des temps sociaux
First published by
Centre de Documentation Universitaire, Paris
Translated and edited by
Myrtle Korenbaum, assisted by Phillip Bosserman

1964

TABLE OF CONTENTS

TRANSLATOR'S PREFACE

American sociologists know Georges Gurvitch as one of the editors of *Twentieth Century Sociology* and as the author of the *Sociology of Law*. His fame in France is confirmed by a long list of publications beginning in 1932 with *Idée du droit social* and *Le temps présent et l'idée du droit social*, followed by *Expérience juridique et philosophie pluraliste du droit* (1936), *La morale théorique et la science des mœurs* (1937, third edition 1961), *Essais de sociologie* (1938), and after the second World War by *La vocation actuelle de la sociologie* (1950, third edition in two volumes 1963), *Les déterminismes sociaux et la liberté humaine* (1955, second edition 1963), *Traité de sociologie* in two volumes (directed by him and to which he made important contributions in 1958, second edition 1963), and finally *Sociologie et dialectique* (1962). In addition a number of courses presented at the Sorbonne have been published in mimeographed form, such as the lectures on the sociological theories of Saint-Simon, Comte, Proudhon and on *The social class concept from Marx till today* (1954, second edition 1960). Translations of these books have appeared in German, Italian, Spanish, Portuguese, Serbian and Japanese.

Georges Gurvitch is recognized as one of the major figures in contemporary sociology.[1] He has been identified as the leading representative of the phenomenological branch of sociological formalism[2], but Gurvitch himself prefers to be known as a representative of dialectical realism, relativism and empiricism. "I have *never* been a partisan of the phenomenology of Husserl, and in fact have always attacked it very violently. My *depth levels* come from Proudhon, Marx and Bergson. Furthermore, I

[1] Don Martindale, *The Nature and Types of Sociological Theory*, Houghton Mifflin Company, Boston, Mass., 1960, pp. 276 ff; René Toulemont, *Sociologie et pluralisme dialectique dans l'œuvre de Georges Gurvitch*, Éditions Nauwelaerts, Louvain, 1950; T. Nogouti, *Étude de la sociologie de Gurvitch*, Tokyo, 1961 (in Japanese); Joseph Gugler, *Die neuere französische Soziologie*, Hermann Luchterhand Verlag, Neuwied, 1961, pp. 110-134.

[2] Don Martindale, *op. cit.*

have *never* been a formalist. On the contrary, formalism has always inspired me with disgust and horror. The German influence arises from Fichte's second period after he had become a realist and from the more contemporary realists Marx, Scheler, Lask and Hartmann... In order to avoid misunderstanding I have now begun to substitute the *manifestations of sociability* for the *forms of sociability*."[1]

Georges Gurvitch was born November 2, 1894 in Novorossisk, Russia. He studied at the University of Petrograd where he was appointed Research Associate in 1917 and Lecturer in 1919. The same year he was appointed Professor at the University of Tomsk, a position which he did not accept. He left Russia in 1920, was named Professor of the Russian section of the University of Prague, Czechoslovakia in 1921. He stayed there three years and then moved on to France where he settled down. He declared his French citizenship in 1928.

From 1927 to 1931 Georges Gurvitch lectured in Paris, first in the Slavic Institute of the University and then at the Sorbonne. He was awarded the Doctorate of Letters in 1932. Appointments were at the *Centre National de la Recherche Scientifique*, College Sévigné, Faculty of Letters at Bordeaux, and full professorship at the University of Strasbourg replacing Maurice Halbwachs (1935–1948).

During World War II he visited the United States. Here he joined the faculty of the New School for Social Research and helped to found the *École Libre des Hautes Études de New York*, which was sponsored by the Provisory Government of Free France. He organized and directed a Sociological Institute in the *École*. While in this country he also held positions as visiting lecturer at Columbia University, Professor of French Area Studies at Rutgers University and ended his stay in the United States as visiting Lecturer at Harvard University.

He returned to France in 1945 to combine a professorship at Strasbourg University with the direction of the Center of Sociological Research which he had founded in Paris. In 1948 he was appointed full Professor of Sociology at the Faculty of Letters and Human Sciences at the University of Paris to fill the chair first occupied by Émile Durkheim. At the same time he became director of studies at the *École Pratique des Hautes Études* (6th section).

[1] Letters to M. Korenbaum from Georges Gurvitch, October 1963.

In 1946 Georges Gurvitch founded the *Cahiers Internationaux de Sociologie* which has published thirty-six volumes to date, and combined this with the direction of the series *Bibliothèque de Sociologie Contemporaine* published by the Presses Universitaires de France. From 1960 to 1963 he was President of the Commission of Sociology and Demography at the *Centre National de la Recherche Scientifique*. In 1962 he was elected President of the International Sociological Association of French Speaking Scholars.

Georges Gurvitch wrote his first Russian thesis on Jean-Jacques Rousseau in 1917. This was followed by a thesis in German on *Fichtes System der konkreten Ethik* in 1924. In France, he studied Durkheim extensively, discussing and working with Marcel Mauss, Lucien Lévy-Bruhl and Maurice Halbwachs. His special interests attracted him to Saint-Simon, Proudhon, and Marx on one hand, and to Bergson, Hauriou, Scheler and Lask on the other hand. His first lectures at the Sorbonne from 1927 to 1931 were dedicated to critical reflections on Husserl's phenomenology, preference being given to realists like Scheler, Hartmann and Lask. These lectures were collected in the volume *Les tendences actuelles de la philosophie allemande*, Paris, Vrin, 1930 (2nd ed., 1948). This book has given some readers the false impression that the author was a follower of the phenomenology which he had actually tried to criticize.

Georges Gurvitch has never isolated himself in an "ivory tower". He has always taken an active interest in political developments and important social experiences. Thus he actively participated in the first stages of the Russian Revolution (1917–1920), in the French labor union movement (1928–1939) served as a soldier at the Maginot line during the second World War (1939–1940), participated in the underground movement against the German occupation and in the United States in the organization of *France Libre*. After his return to France and up to the present time he has continued to participate in the labor union movement. He prefers a pluralistic decentralized collectivism based on workers' self-government (*autogestion ouvrière*).[1] In 1962 he was the victim of a terrorist attentat by the O.A.S. for his public protest against police

[1] See *The Bill of Social Rights*, New York, 1946; *La vocation actuelle de la sociologie*, Vol. II, 1963, pp. 452–461; *Le temps présent et l'idée du droit social*, Paris, Vrin, 1932, pp. 13–99, 213–295.

brutality directed towards the Algerian demonstrators. Gurvitch believes, not without reason, that his sociological theories are far less schematic than they appear, because they are from the beginning founded on living experiences of social reality – its becoming, crises, revolutions, etc.

The extensive variety of his personal social experiences, his political preferences, and the very profound intellect have heightened Gurvitch's sensitivity to the extreme complexity of social reality. It is certainly true that Georges Gurvitch possesses one of the great creative imaginations of twentieth century sociology. He sketches his explanations of social reality in bold strokes and bequeaths to his students a "gold-mine" of material to investigate in more painstaking detail.

The Spectrum of Social Time takes on special significance both in terms of its subject matter and as an introduction to Gurvitch's general theoretical framework. In this work he applies his depth level analysis to social time and brings into clear focus its multi-faceted aspects, the relation of these aspects to various social phenomena and their social frameworks.

Depth level analysis is in direct contrast to the closed, static system of structure-functionalism. It is designed to deal with the open moving drama of social reality, forever in process and changing. It is intended as a guide for a realistic interpretation of complex, fluid, emergent social reality. It treats social reality holistically, even while it permits an analytic examination of the component parts in dynamic movement. Total social reality is so complex there is always a danger of being overwhelmed by the extensive variety of its elements, often conflicting and contradictory.

The internal dilemma which sociology has not adequately resolved is the degree to which it can make comprehensive generalizing statements that are nevertheless empirically valid. Individual sociologists handle this dilemma in a variety of ways; some by so many reservations that the value of generalization is lost; others by confining themselves to so very narrow and limited investigations they leave themselves with little to say for society that is truly significant. But Georges Gurvitch comes to grips with this problem as one that has to be solved before sociology can attain scientific maturity.

It is a mistake to think of this approach as entering into the outdated argument of humanism versus scientism. On the contrary, it is designed to inaugurate a special kind of scientific approach as a substitute for the traditional one which has been inadequate to handle the dynamic complexity of social reality.

It is intended to be utilized pragmatically. Every area that concerns the sociologist can in turn be subjected to an intense scrutiny with this analytic framework for a guide. Gurvitch makes this quite clear. "I aim to show that scientific sociology can only be a reconstruction, which is never fully achieved, of the total social life in action and in movement. It is a reconstruction which ought to be attempted anew for each framework, situation, conjuncture, turning. Even every conceptual apparatus is made and remade, and can only serve as a point of reference. Its validity must be proved pragmatically in an always changing experimentation. This is, moreover, the meaning of 'hyper-empiricism' in sociology. All that sociology can do according to this conception, is to try to reconstruct, starting each time from the points of reference better adapted to apprehending the unanticipated turning of social reality in movement."[1]

Although phenomenological "bracketing" might appear to have some similarity to Gurvitch's depth level analysis, there is a pronounced difference. Whereas phenomenology attempts to "bracket" or strip away successive layers to arrive at the "essence" of the experiencing, intentional consciousness, Gurvitch utilizes the conceptualization of levels as a systematic way to penetrate from the surface of readily observed, objectified social data to the very deepest, most obscure and veiled layers of social reality. No connotation of penetrating to the essential, significant base is involved. The relative importance of any single layer is a matter of the particular phenomenon being examined and its variations.

Gurvitch does not deny the usefulness or validity of the traditional scientific method. He merely notes that there are limitations in our present capacity to handle the deeper, more obscure but nevertheless exceedingly important layers of social reality with the more traditional approach. He therefore proposes the method of hyper-empirical dialectics.[2]

Hyper-empirical dialectics goes beyond the traditional thesis, antithesis and synthesis because it is conceived as movement of social reality,

---

[1] 'Réponse à une critique', *Cahiers internationaux de sociologie* 13 (1952) p. 103.
[2] See 'Hyper-empirisme dialectique' in *Cahiers internationaux de sociologie,* 15 (1953) 3–33, The most recent and complete development appears in *Dialectique et sociologie.* Paris, Flammarion, 1962, pp. 189 ff.

as a multiplicity of ways to find out its turnings and thus includes the following: (1) Dialectics of complementarity: (a) distinctions which veil each other reciprocally. They appear to exclude each other but in reality include each other. (b) Distinctions in parallel or alternating relationship to each other. (c) Distinctions which complete each other. Examples are abstract and concrete, superficial and profound, etc. (d) Direct opposites, such as North Pole and South Pole, the negative and positive poles of electric current, etc. (2) Dialectics of mutual involvement consists in finding those terms which at first glance appear to be opposites but in actuality overlap, as for instance in the duality of body and mind or the mental and social sphere. (3) Dialectics of ambiguity and ambivalence is utilized to penetrate such contrasts as friends who are at the same time enemies, or attractions which at the same time repulse, comforts which menace, etc. (4) The dialectics of polarization is the classical form of dialectics of thesis, antithesis, synthesis. (5) Reciprocity of perspectives is a more intensified form of the dialectics of mutual involvement, but utilized to penetrate distinctions where the immanence of the elements or terms is so intense that it results in a parallelism or symmetry in their manifestations.

Gurvitch emphasizes the distinction between the micro-sociology and macro-sociology. Micro-sociology is concerned with the manifestations of sociability or kinds of relationships which are ways of being bound into the whole and by the whole. There can be $n + 1$ manifestations of sociability, but the most fully conceptualized are Communion, Community and Mass relations. These represent three different intensities of we-nesses. In mass sociability the fusion into we-nesses is weak and at the surface and remains closed at the deeper personal level. In Community the integration takes place at a deeper and more intimate level, while Communion represents the most intense degree of fusion. The bond is most intense in Communion, but is felt as the least constraining and as having the least pressure. At the opposite end of the continuum, Mass we-nesses have the weakest bond and yet are felt as having the greatest pressure. In Communion, in spite of its intensity, the fusion into we-nesses makes the collective and individual aspirations appear to coincide and this is one of the reasons that the pressure is not felt. In unusual events such as wars, revolutions, strikes, catastrophes, Communion bonds may emerge in groups in which Community or Mass bonds ordinarily predominate.

Each group can at special times exhibit intense forms of Communion, or relax into Community or Mass bonds.[1]

Gurvitch recognizes a relation between micro-Sociology and sociometry and sees a potential in the use of sociometric testing and sociodrama to measure the degree of the fusion into we-nesses. He makes some very creative, specific and practically applicable suggestions to expand research in this area.[2] The crucial questions revolve around the conditions for formation or dissolution of the we-nesses, the degrees of intensities of their bonds, how the bonds vary at the symbolic level, the value and attitude level, etc.

Macro-sociology is the study of groups and of global societies, each of which are clusters of the micro-social elements or forms of sociability. This distinction between micro-sociology and macro-sociology permits us to make more perceptive and explanatory analyses of groups. Groups contain within them a cohesion of Communion, Community and Mass bonds, any one of which predominates at a given time or in given social conjunctures. External events or unusual circumstances such as panic or an overt manifestation of prejudice, etc., can upset a cohesion and bring into predominance any one of the forms of sociability that was formerly submerged.

The study of groups proper is the domain of macro-sociology and includes structurable and structural equilibria. The scheme of classification of groups includes fifteen criteria such as size, degree of permanence, rhythm, degree of dispersion, goals to accomplish, modes of admission, etc. This is more than a general scheme. It is useful in that it permits a much keener analysis of group formation and group functioning than has been done till now, as well as a more fruitful study of problems of sociology of knowledge, moral life and law. Finally, it aids in a penetrating empirical analysis of social classes.[3]

It is also possible to treat groups from the micro-sociological stand-

---

[1] Cf. *La vocation actuelle de la sociologie*, Presses Universitaires de France, Paris, Vol. I, 3rd ed., 1963, pp. 119–181 and a short notice in English 'Mass, Community, Communion', *Journal of Philosophy* 38 (1941) 485–496.

[2] See *La vocation actuelle de la sociologie*, *op. cit.*, pp. 249–283 and in English 'Microsociology' in *Sociometry in France and the United States*, Boston, Beacon House, 1950, pp. 25 ff.

[3] Cf. *La vocation actuelle de la sociologie*, *op. cit.*, pp. 285–402 and *Traité de sociologie*, 2nd ed., 1963, Vol. I, pp. 185–204 and Vol. II, pp. 103–206.

point. Which of them fuse to form we-nesses in specific social situations? How profound or how tenuous is this fusion? Under what social conditions do combinations of groups break apart and fuse into new combinations, etc.?

Macro-sociology also deals with the analysis of inclusive or global societies and their structures. Gurvitch defines inclusive societies, as follows: (a) They have sovereignty over all their sectors, collectivities and a juridical sovereignty delimiting the activity of all the functional groupings. The latter includes the State whose political sovereignty is always relative and subordinate. (b) Each global society is not only structurable but also structured. (c) Global society is supra-functional, that is to say it can never be reduced to the totality of its groups, functions or goals. It can never be adequately expressed in any organization taken separately, nor even in the combination of them. (d) In all global societies there is, however, a certain degree of organization, either rudimentary or developed. (e) Inclusive societies participate and help create a civilization, but these are not identical. The types of inclusive societies are more numerous than civilizations. Civilizations are the cement of global structures even while overflowing them. They are in large part products of inclusive societies but they outlive them. There is a dialectic relation between the global society, its structure and the civilization.

Eight criteria for classifying the inclusive social structures are utilized: (a) the hierarchy of groupings; (b) the combination of forms of sociability; (c) which depth levels are accented; (d) ways in which labor is divided and wealth is accumulated; (e) the hierarchy of social control; (f) the cultural products which cement the inclusive social structure; (g) the scale of temporalities.

With this definition of inclusive social structure and utilizing the eight criteria, Gurvitch distinguishes fourteen types of total inclusive societies. Four of these are primitive or archaic social structures. (1) Tribes organized mainly into clans but with fairly important family bands (as found in Australia and among the Indians of South America). (2) Tribes which integrate a variety of groups under a chief with religious powers (as found in Polynesia and Melanesia). (3) Tribes having military, extended family and clan divisions (found among the Indians of North America). (4) Tribes with clan divisions organized into monarchies, in which locality groupings predominate over a profusion of other groupings, and having a theogenic and cosmogenic mythology which intervenes directly in the social structure (as found in North Africa).

There are six historical types of social structures. (1) Charismatic Theocracies (such as in Ancient Egypt). (2) Patriarchal Societies (as described in the Old Testament and the Germanic *Hausgenossenschaft*, etc.). (3) Feudal Societies (in Europe from the tenth to the fourteenth centuries). (4) City-States (as the Greek *Polis* and the Roman *Civitas* from $\pm$ 500–100 B.C.). (5) Societies of Nascent Capitalism. (6) Developed Competitive Capitalism (predominant in Europe in the nineteenth and the beginning of the twentieth century).

The four contemporary societies are: (1) Societies of Developed and Organized Capitalism (U.S.A. is an obvious example). (2) Techno-Bureaucratic Fascist Societies (Italy from 1922 to 1944 and Germany from 1933 to 1945). (3) State Collectivism (U.S.S.R. since 1917 and China since 1949). (4) Pluralistic Collectivism in which Industrial Democracy and Political Democracy are balanced. (This last type has not yet been realized, but Gurvitch sees development in this direction in Jugoslavia and a possibility that U.S.S.R. wil evolve in the same way and even some indications that Great Britain and Sweden may one day take this route).[1]

Distinguishing these types of societies according to the eight criteria enhances the analysis of forces at play in the social structure. Particularly important is the application of depth level analysis. Depth level analysis is not limited to inclusive societies, but is applied to groups and forms of sociability as well. It is one of the key elements of Georges Gurvitch's theoretical framework.

The depth levels are separated for purposes of analysis only. In reality they interpenetrate and reciprocally influence each other. Their relative importance, that is the degree to which certain levels are accented is a matter of the specific social phenomenon in question.

In outline form we can describe these levels as follows: (1) *The ecological surface* includes both the natural and the technological environment. Geographical factors such as climate, topography, quality of soil are included. These factors limit the social sphere and are penetrated by the social as well. Technological items could not be invented or even utilized

[1] See *Déterminismes sociaux et liberté humaine*, Presses universitaires de France, Paris, 2nd ed., 1963, pp. 214–324 and *La vocation actuelle de la sociologie, op. cit.,* Vol. I, pp. 447–507, Vol. II, pp. 431–461.

without the intervention of other layers such as collective values and attitudes, symbols, norms, etc. Demographic data such as birth rate, death rate, marriage rate, population age pyramids, distribution of the population, migrations of population between nations and from rural to urban areas are data of the ecological surface. The material elements of civilization such as buildings, roadways, means of communication are studied at this level. These items can be observed easily, counted, manipulated statistically. These are important factors in the understanding of social reality, but are never to be considered the determining factors. It is obvious that when an attempt is made to determine optimum populations, values and attitudes must be taken into consideration as well as the relation between population number and technological development. Thus this layer is placed first, but it is to be considered first only in terms of its relative accessibility to observation. (2) At the *organizational level* collective conduct is relatively pre-established, stable, hierarchized and centralized according to rules which are fixed in advance. Organization exercises external constraints over individuals and groups, but is not to be confused with social structure.[1] The level of organization is a little more fluid and dynamic than the ecological surface, but more formal and more constraining than the less crystallized levels subjacent to it. There are also variations in the rigidity of organization. Democratic organization is less rigid and more open to the other levels than authoritarian organization, and both of these are less rigid and more open than totalitarian organization. The degree of rigidity depends not only on the measure to which organization is open to and intertwined with the subjacent levels, but also on whether the mystic or rational character predominates. Size is also significant, since organization tends to become more rigid and impersonal as the size of the collectivity increases.

Many groupings that remain unorganized or never attain a unified organization, as for example social classes, would be overlooked if groups and global societies are distinguished in terms of their organization alone. We tend to think of organization as having a determining force, particularly in our current era, because technology and organization have become more and more interwoven. This is manifested in the bureaucratic organization of the state, army, police force, even political parties,

[1] See 'Le concept de structure sociale', *Cahiers internationaux de sociologie* **19** (1955) 3–44 and *La vocation actuelle de la sociologie, op. cit.,* Vol. I, pp. 403–446.

etc. In reality, organization has very different effects on different groups. A hierarchized, centralized type of organization will affect political parties, churches and schools differently. The effects of organization will also vary in critical social conjunctures such as revolutions, economic crises, international or civil wars. Also, kinds of organization do not have an automatic effect, since *men* direct organization and orient their action, not in a vacuum, but in relation to the other depth levels.

There may be real conflict between this level and the ecological level. At least, there is always a relation. For example, when nations prohibit emigration or immigration or when a group retreats from the material world, both the ecological level and the organizational level are relevant.

(3) *Models, rules, signals, signs* and *conduct of relative regularity* make up the next level. The meanings of signals and signs are arrived at by convention and they are intended to guide and direct both individual and collective conduct in a specific social framework. This level includes conduct outside organization which is nevertheless more or less regular. It includes ritual, relatively rigid procedures and practices, routines, mores as well as the more fluid fashions and fads, and even collective conduct which is actually non-conforming. Models, rules, signals, signs are guides, directives and norms which claim validity and demand obedience. They are products as well as producers of culture. They can exert effective pressure on the social reality in which they participate. They are usually recognized as valid guides or proscriptions. Do they continue to remain valid after they have ceased to be obeyed? To answer this question a distinction must be made between technical models, whose validity depends only on repetition and utility, and the cultural models, whose validity derives from ideals and values and which do not depend on utility. Technical models and cultural models always interpenetrate but to varying degrees in different societies or groupings. For instance, economic activity which is basically technical is pervaded by cultural models, while religion, art and education which are basically cultural are helped by technical models. The sociologist studies the efficacy of the cultural and technical models in different social frameworks, where their psychological influence varies. For example, legal prohibitions have differing degrees of influences in Britain, the U.S.A. and France. In Britain abstention is almost total, in the U.S.A. the prohibitions are not always followed and the motivation to obey varies with the type of restriction, while in France abstention

is very uncertain and precarious. These three societies are characterized by very different intensities of efficacy of models, rules and signals.

(4) *Social roles* are dealt with at the next level. Collectivities such as groups, classes and inclusive societies play, assume, and interpret roles just as much as individuals do. Although roles appear to be somewhat stabilized, the individual and collective actors make varied interpretations of how social roles are to be played.

There are roles whose manifestations in conduct can be more or less predicted. On the other hand, some roles cannot be foreseen. Among the roles that can be foreseen are the preferred roles, the virtual roles, and the roles to which individuals and collectivities aspire. Among the roles which cannot be foreseen, that is, the role conduct cannot be predicted, are the imaginary roles, the invented or created roles. In any case there is a dynamism in the realization and interpretation of social roles. Roles have a considerable margin of surprise and spontaneity.

Social roles are influenced by the collective attitudes which are directly subjacent to them. Collective attitudes serve as a basis for the choice of roles that are preferred, that are played and how they will be interpreted.

(5) *Collective attitudes* cannot be reduced to the psychological for they include the imponderables of the social atmosphere, of the total social configurations of which the mental is only one aspect. Collective attitudes can be described as collective configurations which are often more virtual than actual.

Collective attitudes are frameworks for a specific hierarchy of values. Within this framework, values are sometimes accepted, sometimes repudiated or rejected. Collective attitudes appear to be more stable than they often are in reality, for they fluctuate, sometimes explode, and can even be completely reversed into their opposites. Collective attitudes are generally more difficult to grasp empirically then the social roles, which represent a manifest action element.

(6) *Symbols, ideas, collective values and cultural products* are grouped in the next level. All of these depend on the other levels of social reality and partially invade them. For example, we can speak of symbols that are related to organization, models, rules, signs and different types of social roles. Cultural products here signifies language, knowledge, morale, art, religion, law as well as their ideological justifications.

Social symbols only partially express their symbolized content, serving as mediators between their contents and the collective and individual agents who formulate them and to whom they are addressed. One of their fundamental characteristics is that they reveal while veiling and veil while revealing whether they are mystic or rational, intellectual or emotional. They push individuals and collectivities to participate in action, even while they obstruct participation.

Social symbols vary in many ways. It depends on who elaborates or emits them, to whom they are addressed, on specific social conjunctures such as peace, revolution, counter-revolution or war, on whether the symbol dominates the symbolized contents or *vice versa*, on the conscious or unconscious elements, on whether they involve reflection or after-thought, on the degree of their crystallization or flexibility, etc.

In addition to their infinite variety, symbols always risk being exceeded or overreached. They may be interpreted to mean more than was original-ly intended. On the other hand, they may not be sufficient for their task so that one is tempted to speak of their "fatigue". Imagination is more im-portant than action in the symbolic sphere. The complicated embellish-ments of the imagination can frequently obstruct or provide an escape from the symbols. Individuals, groups and societies are not always masters of their own symbols, but easily become victims and slaves of them.

As far as ideas or values are concerned, the sociologist does not have to justify their objective validity nor unmask them. All he need do is to treat them as social data. The collective ideas intended to clarify or justify the movement or advance of collectivities are often rigidified too quickly, and are then passively followed. They impede action when they claim to be self-evident, necessary and eternal. In this form of received ideas they obstruct human intervention.

Collective values can arrest action if they are too easily compromised, if they depend too much on the ideas and symbols, if they become incrusted and incarnated into the *status quo*, if they claim to be eternal or if they pose as predestined and perfect. They then become the strongest obstacle to human intervention in social reality.

(7) *Collective mentality* is the deepest layer and the most difficult to penetrate and objectify. There is no reason to limit mental life to isolated individuals or to their relations with others. The individual mentality, the interpersonal mentality, and the collective mentality are only three di-mensions of the total psychic phenomena.

The three aspects of mental life – mental states (such as representations, memory, suffering or satisfaction), opinions and mental acts (such as intuitions and judgements) are permeated by the social reality, but to differing degrees. The tendency to be open to the social is least characteristic of mental states, somewhat more characteristic of opinions, which are always hesitant and uncertain, and most characteristic of mental acts. Collective mentality varies and fluctuates according to the increasing spontaneity of the relation between mental states, opinions and mental acts.

There is always a danger of tautology in the use of "collective mentality" as an explanatory device, as when a strike is explained as the result of the "aggressive mentality" of the workers, or a revolution as the result of the "revolutionary mentality" of the people. This danger arises when "collective mentality" is thought of as a unified substance.

To summarize this schematic presentation of Gurvitch's theoretical framework, depth level analysis is applied to micro-sociology or the manifestations of sociability and to macro-sociology which includes the groupings, classes and inclusive or global society. Hyper-empirical dialectics is used to sharpen the distinctions that can be made in these areas. Social phenomena are examined within this framework.

Gurvitch himself has already applied this systematic framework for analysis to the Sociology of Law, the Sociology of Knowledge, the Sociology of Ethics and the Sociology of Determinism and Human Freedom. This volume is an application of his method to the study of time.

The Spectrum of Social Time focuses on the complexity of the temporal. We are made aware of the error of treating *time* as a unity, when in fact it is multiple. This is crucial to the sociologist who is involved in attempts to predict and explain. Social roles, attitudes, values, etc. move in their own characteristic *time*. They vary in their durations, in their rhythm, in the degree to which they are dominated by the past or projected into the future, etc.

In English usage, we tend to use *time* in the singular form and this in itself encourages a mental set for an interpretation of time as a unity. It requires intellectual control to strip away this strongly ingrained preconception of time in order to recognize its multiplicity.

To make it easier to grasp Gurvitch's general presentation it would be profitable to introduce concrete examples of how societies have labeled and dealt with time. Modern industrial societies apply numerical designations to both demarcations of point in time and to measures of duration, whereas primitive societies use concrete activities or observable phenomena. It is rather obvious that for primitive societies time designations are communicable within very circumscribed local areas. Hallowell[1], for instance, could not use the typical western meal time referent to make appointments with his Salteaux Indian informants. Meals for them are an individual matter rather than social and are eaten whenever convenient for the individual. He was forced to say "Come as soon as you have lifted your nets", an activity that regularly took place the first thing in the morning but recognizable as a time designation to a very limited local group.

What is not so obvious is the extent to which local areas in modern industrial societies have attempted to control their own time designations. Numerical labels are often credited with an almost magic-like power to impose coordination. However, local groups have often and long resisted attempts to coordinate time designations as required by industrial efficiency. As late as 1860, three hundred local times were observed in the United States. Philadelphia was five minutes slower than New York time and five minutes faster than Baltimore time.[2] On the "day of two noons", Sunday, November 18, 1882, standard time was adopted by the railroads, but it was not until 1918 that Congress made standard time the rule for the entire nation.

That we have not yet achieved coordination in this year of nineteen hundred sixty three is apparent in this quotation from the May 10th issue of *Time Magazine*. "It's time to do something about time. This was the consensus of a parade of witnesses representing transportation, communication, finance and farm who testified before a Senate committee called to consider three bills for reforming the U.S.'s unhappy clock chaos...

Of the 28 states that observe D.S.T. (daylight saving time), only half impose it on a statewide basis, and they all turn it on and off whenever they feel like it. Compounding the confusion are the country's four time

---

[1] A. Irving Hallowell, 'Temporal Orientation in Western Civilization and in a Preliterate Society', *American Anthropology* **39** (1937) 654 ff.
[2] Harrison J. Cowan, *Time and Its Measurements*, Cleveland, The World Publishing Company, 1958, p. 45.

zones. In Indiana, for instance, the boundary between Eastern Standard and Central Standard Time splits the state from north to south. In parts of northern Idaho, Daylight Saving Time is observed on a door-to-door basis. And passengers on the 35-mile bus route between Steubenville, Ohio and Moundsville, W. Va., would, if they wanted to keep local time for all the stops on the way, have to adjust their watches no less than seven times.

Most of the witnesses of last week's Senate Commerce Committee hearing cited the wastefulness and expense of the U.S. time snarl...".

Resistance to time coordination still continues. The latent conflict between rural and urban elements is expressed when Daylight Saving Time is shunned as "city time" and in the outcry against any change as tampering with "God's time."

We can illustrate the interplay of depth levels involved in this problem. (1) At the ecological surface the geographical breadth of the United States, the location of cities and towns that are economically dependent on each other, the daily migration of workers from outlying suburbs to city centers, and the network of communication systems thrust very specific problems on time coordination. (2) At the organization level the requirements of national coordination conflict with democratic organization which implies choice based on local preference. The economic organization and the political organization must come to terms on this issue. (3) Signs and signals are involved in that the hour designations direct the scheduling of daily conduct. Signs and signals are not an individual matter but have to be arrived at by social convention. In this case, confusion results when individuals must behave according to signs and signals which originate from a number of different locality centers. (4) The network of social roles come into play when, for instance, the conduct of the father role is scheduled according to suburb time while the corresponding occupational role must be scheduled according to city time. (5) Collective attitudes are involved in our attitudes toward "clock time". The "clock time" has to be changed in order to take better advantage of daylight. It is much more difficult to schedule everything one hour earlier than it is to move the hands of the clock, because we are bound by our collective attitudes toward clock time. (6) Daylight Saving Time symbolizes to the farmer the dominance of city centers and industrialization in our economy and acts as a "call to arms" for immediate, non-reflective resistance. (7) Collective mentality is reflected in the degree to which notion of the power of human intervention can overcome the mental state of powerlessness to solve complex issues. In the micro-sociological sphere, we can examine the formation of we-nesses among individuals and groups to support the issue of unification of time, as well as the scissions that will arise. At the macro-sociological level one could examine the formation of the Committee for Time Uniformity, the leader-ship of its chairman Robert Ramspeck, the effectiveness of its operation as a pressure group, whether it is a dispersed group, how it attracts its membership, how one gains admission, etc.

The relation of the social framework of time can be illustrated in the adoption of equalized hours to replace the unequal temporal periods. It is an oversimplification to say that this change was the consequence of the technological invention of the mechanical clock. Social factors must have intervened. For example the clepsydra or water clock, in use in India and China as early as 4000 B.C., in Greece through the classical era had to have a system of markings to convert the measurement of the fairly regular flow of water into temporal hours, the length of which changed from season to season. An early Egyptian clock, dated about 1415 to 1380 B.C. has a truncated cone with the temporal hours marked on the inside, each month having separate series of markings to approximate the length of hours correct for the season. The British Museum has on display a small prism two and one half inches by one half inch which has been identified as a portable time calculator for converting equal hours into temporal hours. It is divided into sections and works on a principle of inverse relations.

Why did users of the water clock find it necessary to go to such great lengths to develop systems of calculations to convert hours of equal duration into temporal hours? Why could they not use the more obvious (to us) hours of equal duration?

Even as late as the fifteenth century, according to Nordmann[1] the pendulums of clocks were adjusted each morning and evening to make them divide the night and day into twelve equal parts. How is it possible to say, then, that the determining factor in the shift from the temporal hour to the equalized hour is the invention of the mechanical clock?

In order to explain this change one would have to take into account a

[1] Charles Nordman, *The Tyranny of Time*, London, T. Fisher Unwin, Ltd., 1925.

multiplicity of social aspects: (1) At the ecological surface, the shift from agriculture based economies to industrial based economies, along with the shift in importance of outdoor work to indoor work. The technological invention of the mechanical clock, as well as the perfection of indoor illumination. (2) At the organizational level one would take into account ancient city organization, city-state organization and the feudal hierarchy. (3) Rituals probably shifted from those related to seasonal variation and agriculture to emphasis on daily prayer at specified intervals and so on.

Again, the question of which segment of the society dominates and controls the time scale is dramatically illustrated in the conflict between State and Church to control the calendar and by the reluctance of the Protestant nations to convert from the Julian to the Gregorian calendar. Although most Catholic nations accepted the Gregorian calendar in the late fifteen hundreds, the change was made two hundred years later in England and the United States. This reluctance to accept the more efficient calendar because of the possible symbolic implications is just another detail to underline the relation of the social framework to the time scale.

In *The Spectrum of Social Time*, Georges Gurvitch has given us a profound and detailed analysis of this relationship, distinguishing different kinds of time, their unification into scales or hierarchies, and the relation to manifestations of sociability, groupings, classes, and different types of inclusive societies. He demonstrates here the rich possibilities of the use of depth analysis and hyper-empirical dialectics. From this study alone we can recognize the potential usefulness of this theoretical framework for the study of social phenomena.

We must acknowledge and express thanks for the very valuable assistance from Don Martindale, Robert Bailey III, and Wsevolod Isajiw.

Myrtle Korenbaum

Northern Illinois University, DeKalb, Illinois
November 1963

CHAPTER I

INTRODUCTION

GENERAL THEORETICAL ORIENTATION

We can take as "given" the fact that social reality is studied not only by the sociologists, but also by representatives of the autonomous social sciences established prior to sociology. To define sociology, both its domain and its method must be made precise.

The domain of sociology is social reality, this mutual participation of collectivities and their members in each other and in a whole, not reducible to any other reality. Social reality is affirmed first and above all in the "total social phenomena", a totality in movement, an ebb and flow of volcanic eruption, a reservoir of the gushing of action and of collective effort. We-nesses, groups, classes and global societies are forced to struggle perpetually against external and internal obstacles. They are created and modified by the total social phenomena and produce multiple human meanings which penetrate them or are grafted on them. Their works are not limited to the cultural and technical products of civilization, the material products transforming the morphological-ecological milieu, but include their "structure", the precarious equilibria of multiple hierarchies. Added to that are organization, patterns, differentiated activities, which express very partially and very inadequately the subjacent totalities. These are always in the process of being made, undone, and remade. The movements of "total social phenomena" have varied intensities: they can precede or trail behind the products of civilization and corresponding structures. The whole of social reality, which cannot be broken down, always takes precedence over all of its particular manifestations; it is ontologically present before all its expressions, works and crystallizations and is never entirely alienated by any of them.

Total social phenomena are *pluri-dimensional*, constituted by stages, layers or depth levels. These depth levels can serve as points of reference for the reconstruction of their indissoluble unity. The sociologist who desires to apprehend total social phenomena proceeds by stages, that is to say, going from the most accessible to the least accessible (this has no evaluative connotation). He may take the following course. He can descend from the ecological surface, which can be grasped by external observation, to the organizations, sometimes ponderous, sometimes lively, but always requiring an hierarchy of functions. Next he arrives at the social patterns, including the collective signals and signs, as well as the rules. These rules are not always tied to organization and often even overflow social structures. He would then reach effective collective behavior, with varied degrees of regularity, embracing rites and procedures, flexible daily practices, fluid and changing fashions and fads, and finally insubordinate, unexpected, non-conforming collective behavior.

Digging deeper, he would discover that collective behavior of varied regularity has as its foundation the network of social assumed and interpreted roles which include those played by the ensembles (the We's, groups, classes), as well as those played by the individuals who participate in them. These various springboards of possible collective and individual action, which sometimes only realize the expected, sometimes innovate and modify the social frameworks in which they act, rests on a subjacent dynamic layer: the collective attitudes which can never be reduced to the psychological. It is a matter of social configurations, more virtual than actual, which encircle a collective mentality of emotional preferences and dislikes, of predispositions to act and react, of tendencies by groups and their members to assume specific social roles, of frameworks where social symbols are manifested and where the collective values are accepted or repudiated.

The social symbols, signs which only partially express the intended contents, serve as mediators between the contents and the collective and individual agents who formulate them and to whom they are addressed. To uncover them beneath the attitudes, the two poles that all social symbols possess must be taken into account. They are both inadequate expressions and incomplete vehicles of participation. Whether predominantly intellectual, emotional or spontaneous, whether tied to the mystic or the rational, the symbols characteristically reveal while veiling and veil while revealing, and while inspiring participation also restrain it. In certain respects all the layered stages of social reality have the characteristics of symbols since they symbolize the indissoluble character of social reality, the total social phenomena, for which they are partial, incomplete, inadequate substitutes. At the same time the splits of the divergent and conflicting depth levels are continually filled by special symbols which infiltrate between them like a fluid social cement.

Generally speaking the social symbols become closely attached to the non-technical products of civilization, such as language, education, knowledge, morality, art, literature, religion, law, etc. Furthermore in order to be valid, the social symbols must lean on already realized collective institutions, both actual and virtual, which transcend the symbolic sphere and yet render them possible. This is true of all substitutes, particularly all signs. It is also necessary that social symbols which have become "tired", dissipated and inefficient, should be replaced.

One arrives next at collective behavior, innovating, creative and effervescent. Here innovation, choice, invention, collective decision and creation are partially exposed to view. These degrees of human freedom are always virtually present in the social reality. Effervescent, innovating, and creative collective behavior is most easily observable at the moment structural changes are provoked by political and social revolutions, or during exceptional historical events, such as a great jolt in religious life, civil and international wars, mass migrations, discoveries of new continents and their civilizations. At these moments "acts" predominate over "products", overturn the established hierarchies of organization patterns, roles, and symbols and create them entirely anew. However, effervescent, innovating and creative collective behaviors are always present and effective in social reality, but with varied degrees of intensity. From this point of view, the forces for conservation and the forces for innovation play out a sharp drama in all total social phenomena. Or more directly a sharp drama is played between the permanent revolution and the not less permanent counter-revolution. It is thus that innovating and creative behavior reverberates in all the depth levels and provokes in them reactions and resistances; thus creative conduct triumphs only under certain conditions.

Collective ideas and values inspire both the collective conduct and the resistance that it encounters. This is another level of social reality. Behind all types of collective behavior and attitudes, all organization, all patterns, signs, roles and symbols, a whole world of collective ideas and values can be discovered. For example, a primitive tribe externalizes its collective attitudes by certain behavior, certain gestures, certain patterns, signs and symbols, weapons, ornaments, clothes, emblems, masks, cries, songs, dances, etc. Whether these are expressions of religious, magical, juridicial or military inspirations, whether they invite exchange transactions, whether they are greetings of welcome or threat, cannot be discovered directly. Only a grasp of the values and ideas involved in these manifestations can settle the question. Similarly, the class struggle is also a struggle between fundamental ideas and values.

But these collective ideas and values must be grasped, defined, and known precisely. This leads the sociologist to the last depth level of social reality, that of the collective mentality or "collective consciousness". The "collective consciousness" is part of the social reality in which it is integrated. From the sociological point of view, it does not possess priority, but constitutes one, among many, of the levels of total social phenomena. Depth sociology considers all psychic facts, conscious or not, that it discovers in social reality, to be situated in being and, more particularly, in collective being. It considers consciousness to be no less immanent to the society, the world and being, than they are immanent to it.

From this point of view, the psychic in general and the consciousness in particular, are realities embedded in other realities. This reciprocal immanence and this tendency to open up are reduced to a minimum in the collective "mental states", as, for example, in representations, memory, sufferings, and the satisfactions, inclinations and efforts. They are moderate in the collective "opinions" which always are hesitant and uncertain. They attain their maximum in the collective "mental acts" which are intuitions of intellectual, emotional and voluntary coloration and judgments. These three degrees of the psychic, as well as the psychic itself, have varied and relative importance in social reality, as they depend on the character of the social framework, total social phenomena, as well as on structures and conjunctures to which the former give birth. This is equally true of the relation between interpersonal and intergroup social mentality, and the individual mentality. As a matter of fact these directions towards *Ours* (We-ness, group, class, global society), *Yours* and *Mine* play a very different role in diverse total social phenomena. These three directions are sometimes found in reciprocity of perspectives, sometimes polarized, sometimes in relations of complementarity, ambiguity, or mutual involvement. However, in all cases, important sectors of the total social phenomena unquestionably lie outside the psychic phenomena. The ecological

4

surface, organizations, technical patterns and objects, social regulations, the products of civilization, and, of course, the social structures are never reduced to the psychic, even the collective psychic.

Depth level analysis of social reality never involves an assessment of the value or the effectiveness of these layers, neither their hierarchical arrangement nor their intensity, inasmuch as they vary according to the character of the social framework. These are a question of fact only. All these depth levels form an indissoluble whole in the total social phenomena. They serve only as points of reference in order to reconstitute the interpenetrated units. A perpetual movement back and forth among the levels is revealed. The levels tend to move in the same direction, but this does not rule out a certain discontinuity and the possibility of tensions, divergencies and conflicts between them.

Finally, depth analysis in revealing the exceptional richness of social reality, represents the triumph of a super-relativism and a consequent empiricism. This exposes to the clear light of day the virtual explosive quality of social reality as a function of these frameworks, and explains why a different conception of the character of social facts can arise in each total social phenomenon.

Total social phenomena are not only pluri-dimensional; it would be an error to identify them always with global society. Micro-social phenomena – the *We-nesses* (Masses, Communities, Communions), the particular groupings, the social classes – are also total social phenomena. Thus, there is a horizontal pluralism as well as a vertical pluralism. The two intertwine. The manifestations of sociability, or the multiple ways of being tied to and by the whole, clash and combine in different degrees of actuality and virtuality in all genuine social unity. The *We-nesses* themselves have depth levels, which are extremely flexible. This flexibility of the depth levels diminishes with the social classes and the global societies which are macrocosms of groupings, at the same time as they are macrocosms of We-nesses. All these social microcosms and macrocosms represent totalities with depth levels of their own.

The wealth of total social phenomena can be revealed in its plenitude only if the fact is taken into account that there are quasi-infinite degrees of "totalization". Moreover, a perpetual drama is played between the partial and global total phenomena. These, at the same time, can be complementary, in a situation of mutual involvement, ambiguous, polarized and in a

5

reciprocity of perspectives. This complex dialectic played between the different frameworks and scales of total social phenomena is as important as that of the depth levels and offers a second point of reference to grasp the dynamic social totalities.

Finally, when real collective units (groups, classes, global societies) are considered as total social phenomena an intense clash is observed between the astructural, structurable, and structured elements, completed by the conflict between the spontaneous and the organized. This latter itself is only one of the elements of equilibrium constituting a structure.[1] This clash is not observed when We-nesses and relations with others are taken as total social phenomena. They are astructural *par excellence*. Included in an incessant dynamic structuration, destructuration or explosion, the structures maintain strained relations with the subjacent total social phenomena, while groups and social classes are in conflict with the global society where they are integrated. It is in this dialectic movement that the exceptional richness of the total social phenomena and vitality of social reality with its dynamic, infinitely complex tensions are here manifested.[2]

This vast field of exploration is the domain of social reality. Three different methods of approach can be used in its study.

1. Using a systematic and analytic method it is possible to pursue practical goals concentrating on a single depth level, more or less artificially detached from the totality, in order to draw the maximum yield and effectiveness in a specific social framework. Here the basic presuppositions are not usually rendered conscious. Such is the procedure in most of the special social sciences. For example, the "science of law", in the technical sense only takes into consideration the patterns and abstract symbols of law, systematized in order to facilitate application by the tribunals and administrative services of a given country. Grammar systematizes the signs and symbols of one language, in order to facilitate its diffusion and

---

[1] Cf. my analyses of social structures in the following: 'Le concept de structure sociale' in *La vocation actuelle de la sociologie*, Vol. I, 3rd ed. 1963, Chapter 6, pp. 403–447; 'Les structures sociales' in *Traité de sociologie*, Vol. I, 2nd ed. 1963, Section II, Chapter 4, pp. 205–215; 'Structures sociales et systèmes de connaissances' in *Notion de structure, XXe semaine de la Synthèse*, Paris, 1957, pp. 281–342; 'Structures sociales et multiplicité des temps', *Bulletin de la Société Française de Philosophie*, 52 (1958) no. 3, Paris, Librairie Colin, 1960, pp. 99–142.

[2] Cf. my analyses in *Dialectique et sociologie*, Paris 1962, Second Part, Chapter I and II, pp. 177–221.

its instruction in a special circle. Geography, while physical remains human and thus social, does not go beyond the ecological level of social reality when it describes the contours, climate, populations, soils and resources related to a specific social framework. Classical political economy analyzes and systematizes certain economic patterns and certain regular collective behavior relating the most efficient production and the most advantageous exchange in order to indicate the best means of achieving prosperity in a determined social framework. The possible variations often escape the economists.

2. The second method of approach to social reality may be described as *individualizing* or *singularizing*. This approach is characteristic of two special social sciences, history and ethnography which, like sociology, study social phenomena as a totality. But ethnography has certain difficulties when moving from structure to total social phenomena. This is because it has to deal with non-promethean societies; that is, societies unaware of possible changes and social upheavals that can result from concerted human action. History, on the contrary, succeeds much better than sociology in following the vicissitudes of the structures and their restructuration and destructuration linked to the movement of their subjacent social phenomena. Historiography, in so far as it is a science, studies promethean (or historic) societies, in what is not repeated and is unique, placing their singularized movement in a continuity of time. However, history itself reveals multiplicity and varied unifications. Here, as I shall show in this book[1] historians and sociologists meet and complement each other. Historians describe the particularly rich variations of historical time and their unifications, while sociologists furnish the historians with indispensable conceptual tools to enable them to grasp the concrete expression of the multiplicity of time and to remind them of the limitations of the continuity between the different time scales to which they are propelled by their reconstructive, projective and singularizing method. Neither history nor sociology possesses a monopoly of the study of social time; they have complementary approaches to it.

3. The third approach to the study of social reality is the *qualitative and*

[1] Also consult my other writings on this subject: 'Continuité et discontinuité en histoire et en sociologie' in *Annales*, Paris 1957, pp. 73–84; 'La crise de l'explication en sociologie' in *La vocation actuelle de la sociologie*, 2nd ed. 1963, Vol. II, pp. 462–481; 'Les règles de l'explication en sociologie' in *Traité de sociologie*, 2nd ed., Paris, 1963, Vol. I, Section II, Chapter 6, pp. 231–251, and *Dialectique et sociologie*, 1962, pp. 224–237.

discontinuous typology of sociology. To be fruitful, this methodology must be linked on the one hand with the awareness of the totalization process, to retain unity as well as multiplicity and on the other hand, to an empirical dialectic. Only the dialectic approach can frustrate all attempts to mummify the typologies.

1. The typological method is as different from the generalizing method of the natural sciences, as from the analytic-systematizing method of most of the specific social sciences, or from the singularizing method of history and ethnography. In sociology typological, discontinuous and qualitative types, which can however be repeated, are constructed. Thus this method generalizes within certain limits, but only in order to bring out more clearly the specificity of type. In constructing the different types as a function of the variety of real social frameworks and their structures, this method singularizes to a certain extent; again, only to get a better hold on the frameworks which are repeatable. It utilizes the data of history, but only in order to accentuate the discontinuity, indeed even the ruptures between the we-nesses, groups, classes, and global societies, on the one hand, and between the subjacent total social phenomena and their superposed structures on the other.

This method presupposes comprehension of the totalities and their meanings, but to the end of making the meanings immanent elements in the moving totalities. Systematizations offered by the particular social sciences are returned to at times, but only as so many points of departure for research into subjacent depth levels. This demonstrates how relative each cohesion of patterns, symbols, and significations is to the particularity of the total social phenomenon. In sociology, the typological method makes sense only when applied to the totalities and their structures. These types are not elaborated in order to establish images of "Epinal", atrophied semblances, or "ideal types" (Max Weber). They are not divided up into "phenotypes" and "genotypes" (Kurt Lewin). They represent dynamic frames of reference adapted to the total social phenomena and are called on to promote explanation in sociology.

It suffices to take into account that sociological types are intermediate between generalization, singularization and systematization, between explanation and comprehension, between repetition and discontinuity, to say that these types can not profitably be constructed without resorting to the dialectic. This is confirmed when the three types are distinguished;

the micro-social, particular groupings such as social classes, and global societies. These are often confused, but in reality they are sometimes complementary, sometimes mutually involved, sometimes polarized, and sometimes symmetrical (in relation to reciprocity of perspectives).[1]

(a) The micro-social types are the types of social bonds (We-nesses, relations with Others), or otherwise stated, of "manifestations of sociability". These are types of astructural total, social phenomena which are actualized, combined and in conflict with each other in the most varied ways within each group, no matter how small, as well as within each global society. The micro-social types are the most *abstract* types and the most general, for they tend towards frequent repetition within the micro-social frameworks.

(b) The types of particular groupings are types of total social phenomena constituting real but partial collective unities (single or multifunctional in nature), which are structurable or structured. These types are more concrete than the micro-social types but less concrete than the types of global societies and social classes. In effect, the repetition of these types in diverse global frameworks produces different forms (e.g. the *clan* in primitive societies, the *domestic family* in patriarchal societies and the *household* in contemporary societies).

(c) The types of social classes and global societies are types of suprafunctional, total social phenomena representing macrocosms of particular groupings. These types are the most concrete and the closest to historical existence; that is to say, they are only rarely repeatable. As classes and global societies are always structured, it is much easier to construct their types by examining their structures, so much the more so because the corresponding total social phenomena are so rich in content.

Distinguishing the three sociological types (abstract or microsocial, abstract-concrete where groupings are concerned, concrete where global societies and social classes are concerned), leads to the following conclusions: (a) They serve as points of reference for their successive construction, while mutually assisting each other for their reciprocal verification. The three types are in dialectic relations of complementarity, of mutual involvement or reciprocity of perspectives..., without excluding the possibility of polarizations of different intensities.

[1] Cf. for greater detail, *La vocation actuelle de la sociologie*, 3rd ed. 1963, Vol. I pp. 11–14, 119–196, 308–402, 458–507.

(b) The comprehension or the direct grasping of the whole and the significations which are a part of it is emphasized more in the construction of social types of global societies and social classes. It is in the global societies and social classes that the problems of cultural meanings are more intensely involved. The types of social bonds and particular groups are constructed more easily. (c) The intensity and respective importance of the depth levels, as well as astructural and structural elements are essentially variable. The hierarchy of groupings is overturned according to the subjacent types of structures and total social phenomena. Also the scales of social determinisms which cause changes in the global societies is different according to these types. For example, in the bourgeois and capitalist society, the determinism of economic and technical patterns has played a role of major importance in every change. It is not at all certain that in other types of societies the ecological and particularly the demographic base, the magical and religious beliefs (or their conflict), law, knowledge, morality or rational planning etc., would not or could not be placed at the head of the social determinisms. Only the specific unification of these constitutes sociological determinism.

2. The second aspect of the sociological method consists in always taking into consideration all the levels, all the scales and all the astructural, structurable and structured sectors of social reality and directly applying to them a view of the whole. Seen from this perspective, the best sociological method is the dialectical method. As a matter of fact, how can we study the going and coming, the interpenetration and tension between the layers, between the scales (we-nesses, groups and global societies), between astructural, structurable and structured elements, between the spontaneous and the organized, between the movements of structuration, destructuration, and restructuration, between the individual and society, all indissolubly linked together and in virtual and actual conflict, without recourse to the dialectical approach? Is it not in submitting all the elements to the dialectical test of complementarity, mutual involvement, ambiguity or reciprocity of perspectives that we can obtain a concrete image of social reality and its types in the process of becoming and disintegrating.[1]

From this point of view, nothing better illustrates the difference be-

---

[1] Cf. my *Dialectique et sociologie*, 1962, pp. 11–28, 176–276.

tween sociology and the specific social sciences than the special branches of sociology themselves: sociology of economics, human ecology or demography, industrial sociology, sociology of law, of language, of knowledge, of religion, social psychology, etc. And, if, as in the approach of the specific social sciences, these special branches of sociology emphasize one level or sector of social reality they make every effort to go beyond. They always end by linking their point of departure to all the other levels; that is to say they integrate it into the total social phenomenon, its frameworks and its movement. The dialectic here prevails over the systematic and prepares the way for explanation.

3. We have described elsewhere in a more precise fashion the third aspect of the sociological method, therefore we refer to the studies devoted to this question for a more detailed analysis.[1]

We believe we have now presented the essential elements for our definition of sociology. Sociology is the qualitative and discontinuous typology based on the dialectic of the total social phenomena in all their astructural, structurable and structured manifestations. It studies all the depth levels, scales and the sectors directly with the aim of following their movements of structuration, destructuration and restructuration and rupture, finding their explanation in collaboration with history.

If a shorter definition is desired, it could be said that *sociology is a science which studies total social phenomena as a totality of their aspects and their movements, capturing them in a dialectic of microsocial, group and global types, in the process of becoming and disintegrating.*

Out of this dynamic conception of sociology, emerges the problem of time in which the life of the social frameworks, total social phenomena and their products, and particularly their structures unfolds. This problem is absolutely primary to sociology. The social structures themselves are not stable, but are discovered, on the contrary, to be involved in a perpetual movement. Moreover, the scale of social time wherein they move is very often divergent from the time scale in which the subjacent total social phenomena live. The latter can always cause eruptions in the structures, sometimes as ignited material, as a volcanic force ready to erupt; sometimes, on the contrary, as a heavy weight slowing down the movement. In

[1] Cf. my *Dialectique et sociologie*, 1962. To add to the pages already quoted: pp. 96–178. Cf. also *La vocation actuelle de la sociologie*, 2nd ed. 1963: 'Philosophie et sociologie', Chapter XVII, pp. 482–496.

another connection and more generally speaking, the multiplicity of social times and the diversity of scales in which they are arranged must be taken into account in order to analyze the problem of sociological determinisms partial and global, which unify the multiplicity of social determinisms in formulas which are not universal and vary with each type of group, class, and global society. We were persuaded of this while writing the book *Les Déterminismes sociaux et la liberté humaine* (Paris, 1955; second revised edition, 1963[1]). In that volume we only treated this problem in passing; we did not go very deeply into the matter. This is why we decided to devote a special public lecture course to this subject. The contents of that course are reproduced in this book. We hope that it will clarify, in a somewhat new way, our conception of the problems belonging to general sociology and our interpretation of the relationships between sociology and history. Finally, the distinction which we introduce here between real social time, the "becoming aware of these times" on the part of collectivities (their grasping, perception, symbolization, conceptualization and their quantification of time) and the efforts of these collectivities to master the times in unifying scales, is meant to serve both sociology of knowledge[2] and general sociology.

Certainly we are not the first to treat the problem of social time which confronts sociology. But the well-known sociologists who have approached this topic, Émile Durkheim, Marcel Mauss, Lucien Lévy-Bruhl, Maurice Halbwachs, and more recently Pitrim Sorokin[3], have not seen all sides of thend have been influenced too ofte problem an by particular philosophical positions. We have attempted in this book to approach the study in such a way as to avoid every preconception. Our sole aim is to show how crucial this problem of time is for sociology and its theory.

[1] In this new edition we did take into consideration the results of the present study.
[2] Concerning the sociology of knowledge see our 'Problèmes de la sociologie de la connaissance' in *Traité de sociologie*, Vol. II, Paris, 1960, Section VII, Chapter II, pp. 103–136; 'La sociologie de la connaissance' in *Année sociologique*, Third Series, Paris, 1949; 'Structures sociales et systèmes de connaissances' in *La notion de structure*, XXe Semaine de la Synthèse, Paris, 1957, pp. 291–342; *Initiation aux recherches sur la sociologie de la connaissance*, Paris, C.D.U., 1948, Casc. I (mimeographed).
[3] See E. Durkheim and M. Mauss, 'Quelques formes primitives de classification' in *L'Année sociologique*, Paris, 1901, 1902, Vol. VI; E. Durkheim, *Les formes élémentaires de la vie réligieuse*, Paris, 1922 ; M. Halbwachs, *La mémoire collective*, (posthumous), Paris, 1950, pp. 103–129; P. Sorokin, *Socio-Cultural Causality, Space and Time*, Durham, 1943.

THE RELATION OF SOCIOLOGICAL THEORY TO STUDY OF TIME

In this book we shall try to show that social life always takes place in divergent and often contradictory manifestations of social time. Difficult as it may be, every society must attempt to unify, even if only relatively, these multiple manifestations of time and attempt to arrange them in a hierarchy. This is unavoidable since each partial element of the global or all-inclusive society tends to move in its own time. These partial elements include the social classes, specific groups, microsocial elements (we-nesses and the relations with others), as well as the depth levels of social reality from the ecological base to collective mentality and even each social activity (mythical, religious, magical, economic, technical, juridical, political, cognitive, ethical, educational). Each of these tends to move in its own time. A society cannot survive without some unification of the plurality of its social time, yet special problems emerge in the very effort to achieve some consistency in this matter. Every all-inclusive society tries to establish a unifying hierarchy of social time. Maurice Halbwachs has already pointed out, for example, the clash in the time dimensions of the family, school, factory, union, administrative office, etc. Patriarchal societies, feudal societies, the ancient city, capitalistic and collectivistic societies tried to harmonize their varied times in divergent ways. All this adds to the complexity of social time. If this multiplicity of social time were clearly pointed out, each formula of sociological determinism would be recognized as valid only for a specific type of society, for a single class or group, and as a consequence would be multiplied.

My research of *Déterminismes Sociaux et Liberté Humaine* (2nd. ed., 1963) led me to investigate the multiple manifestations of social time. I constructed eight different kinds of social time as frames of reference for sociological analysis:

1. Enduring Time (time of slowed down long duration).
2. Deceptive Time (where under an apparent calm, sharp crises produce a time of surprise.)
3. Erratic Time (time of irregular pulsation between the appearance and disappearance of rhythms, the time of uncertainty).
4. Cyclical Time (in which past, present and future turn in a circle).
5. Retarded Time (which is too long awaited).
6. Alternating Time (time alternating between delay and advance).

7. Time pushing forward (which makes the future actually present).

8. Explosive Time (explosive time of creation).

These eight kinds of time were employed by me in the description of different types of social and sociological determinisms without further elaboration. But I reached the conclusion that the *multiplicity of social time* has great sociological significance for three different reasons.

(a) In the first place, each social framework and, more particularly each global society cannot be analyzed without placing it in time. When nations and civilizations (French, British, American, German, Occidental, Oriental, etc.) confront each other directly, the differences of their social time become apparent and grave errors are committed if they are not correctly delineated. Time in France is not identical with time in Norway, nor with time in Brazil. The tempo of the French Revolution differed from that of the Russian Revolution.

(b) In the second place, the multiplicity of social time is a central problem of the sociology of knowledge. In this branch of sociology, the different kinds, forms and systems of knowledge are in functional correlation to their corresponding social frameworks. This raises the question of the variety of ways to grasp intuitively, perceive, symbolize and know time in the different social frameworks. There are two aspects to the multiplicity of social time: on the one hand, the many ways of becoming aware of time in the different social frameworks and on the other, the multiple manifestations of the real time in which the social frameworks move.

(c) In the third place, there is the problem of the validity of social determinisms and their unifications which vary with each type of group, class and global society. This is linked, as has already been indicated, to the problem of the multiplicity of social time.

In *The Psychology of Time*, (1957), Paul Fraisse has suggested that all research on time is divided into three aspects: (a) *the conditioning of time;* (b) *the perception of time;* (c) *the mastery of time.* On the whole, this division is acceptable. Furthermore, the above three reasons for the sociological significance for research into multiple time are somewhat analogous to the distinctions made by Fraisse. Only it is necessary to state explicitly that time is not conditioned by external conduct, but by the social framework, and, to sum it up, by the *total social phenomena* in their global, group and microsocial aspects. Furthermore, the "conditioning of time" is never unilateral for us. It is reciprocal because the social frameworks

14

condition time as well as being conditioned by it. We have already noted, generally speaking, that since the movements which produce time also take place in time, by this fact they are partially produced by time. Here we meet dialectics again.

It is not sufficient to speak of the perception of time. One must also speak about grasping time intuitively, representing it and symbolizing it, knowing and measuring it, and finally, quantifying it. That is why we prefer the expression "to become conscious of time". Finally, Fraisse places the "estimation, conceptualization and quantification of time" under the rubric of the *mastery of time*. We have some reservations about this, since we believe that time can be estimated, conceptualized, and known without always being *mastered*.

At least according to the meaning we have given the term, mastery means *to unify time* in a definite manner. This definition does not exclude the fact that the effort to quantify social time (an effort whose success is often problematic) should not be considered under the aspect of the struggle for the *mastery of time*, or as entering into the effort to master time. Again, Fraisse only admits the "diversity of temporal horizons" which appears to us to be too subjective. We shall try to show without circumlocution *the reality of the multiple manifestations of time* and especially *the reality of the multiple manifestations of social time*. We prefer the statement "the reality of movements and the time which they produce" rather than the ambiguous "conditioning of time".

We have contraposed the psychologist's points of view only in order to make the problems we are going to encounter more precise. Certainly there are a number of questions which can be raised, and they will probably come at us from all directions.

(1) What do you mean by *time*? Are you partisan to a particular philosophy of time? Do you intend to submit the sociology of time to a preconceived philosophical position?

(2) Is the *multiplicity of time* generally possible? Does it not destroy time both as reality and as an element experienced or grasped? Does it not destroy time as a concept?

(3) What do you mean by *social time*? How do you distinguish it from psychological time on the one hand, and from time of the external world on the other hand. Furthermore, is the social time you speak of *real time*, the time constructed as an operational concept of sociology, or also time

15

experienced, grasped, perceived, represented, symbolized and quantified? Can some of these time manifestations be mastered?

(4) How can the social time studied by sociology be distinguished from the social time studied by history? Or, more precisely, is there a difference between sociological time and historical time? If the answer is yes, what are the points of this difference? This last question will be answered in Chapter II.

We cannot proceed with this analysis until we have answered in detail the questions formulated above. Therefore Chapter II will be devoted to these matters where we take up the general considerations of the multiple manifestations of time.

To reassure the readers about the sociological contents of this book we shall now present an outline of the material we intend to cover.

Chapter II will be devoted to specifying what we mean by time and also by social time and to distinguishing the various kinds of social time. A special section will deal with sociological time and historical time. Chapter III will point out the different kinds of social time where the different depth levels of social reality tend to unfold. These depth levels are the ecological base, organizations, the models and the patterns of conduct, the network of social roles, the collective attitudes, symbols, ideas, collective values, and finally the collective mentality. Thus the second chapter will be entitled, 'The Problem of Time', the third, 'The Depth Levels and Social Time'.

Four chapters will deal with multiple manifestations of social time in correlation with real social frameworks and their types. Thus Chapter IV will be entitled: 'The Microsocial Frameworks and their Social Time'. In this chapter the we-nesses and relations with others, such as Masses, Communities, and Communions, the interpersonal and intergroup relations dealing with approach, withdrawal and mixed relations will be considered relative to the social time in which they tend to move.

Chapter V, 'The Particular Groupings and their Social Time', will be devoted to both structured and non-structured groupings distinguished according to the degree of their dispersion (groupings at a distance, groupings of artificial contact, groupings meeting periodically, and permanent intimate groupings). We shall also study groupings distinguished according to the mode of admission, their orientation, their functions (kinship groupings, fraternal, locality, economic activity, non-profit

16

activities, and mystic-ecstatic groupings) and the *manifestations of social time in which they tend to move.*

In Chapter VI, 'The social Classes and their Scales of Time'. we shall examine the peasantry, the bourgeoisie, and the proletariat from the point of view of the social time in which they move and the hierarchies of time which they produce.

In Chapter VII and VIII, *Global Societies and their Scales of Time,* the problem of the possible conflict between the scales of social time belonging to a global structure and the scale of time characteristic of the subjacent total phenomena will be raised.

It is easy to see from this outline that in these eight chapters we shall re-examine the problems of general sociology that we have discussed in the two volumes of *La vocation actuelle de la sociologie* (Vol. I, 3rd ed., 1963; Vol. II, 2nd ed., 1963) and in *Traité de sociologie* (Vol. I, 2nd ed., 1963). However, they will be approached from a new angle: that of the multiple manifestations of social time and their varied unifications.

We are now ready to answer the four questions referred to in our introduction:

(1) What do we mean by the concept of time? (2) Is the multiplicity of time possible? (3) Exactly what is signified by "social time" and the multiple manifestations of social time? Are they real times, experienced and grasped, or symbolized, conceptualized, or quantified times? (4) What is the difference between sociological and historical time?

CHAPTER II

THE PROBLEM OF TIME

To specify what we mean by time, it is sufficient to define it as *convergent and divergent movements which persist in a discontinuous succession and change in a continuity of heterogenous moments*. This delimitation places time outside mere philosophical theories of time. The sociologist cannot participate in the arguments over the justification nor the abolition of time in favor of eternity which many philosophers from Parmenides and Plato to Hegel have been tempted to do. As a matter of fact, the theories of the "Living eternity" of Plotine, Saint Augustine, Schelling and Hegel, who reduce human time to divine time, only seem to present the most diffused formulas for the destruction of real time in eternity. Our descriptive definition of time also avoids taking a position on the subject of the primacy of ontological time or of "consciousness of time". There was a long tradition of identifying time with the "consciousness of time", and the "consciousness of time" with individual consciousness (Janet). Even philosophers who have revolutionized the interpretation of the "consciousness of time" by rendering it problematic, as Bergson and Husserl have done, have not been able to break away from idealistic subjectivism. That is why, in *Les données immediates de la conscience*, Bergson spoke of the "qualitative duration as seen exclusively by the deeper self" (even when it is understood as a submerged self), and why Husserl reduced the problem of time to that of the "phenomenology of the interiority of the consciousness of time".

However, in *Matière et mémoire* and in *L'évolution créatrice* Bergson accounts for the entire world process in terms of different degrees of the "depth of the qualitative duration", which for him represents effective time, and takes a clearly realistic position in regard to time. Perhaps a clear affirmation that consciousness is immanent to being, and that the first always opens to the last, would end the philosophers' hesitations between the subjective and objective interpretations of time. For my part, I am inclined to consider both of these interpretations erroneous and outmoded. But this is not directly pertinent to this study.

18

The above definition of time to which I am committed attempts to avoid the philosophical issue and also by-passes Aristotle's classical conception, according to which *time is a measure of movement* (this presupposes that all time can be reduced to measure, and, since the measures are integrated into a unity, there is only one single time). It also by-passes Saint Augustine's conception ("I know what time is if one does not ask me") which has contemporary supporters. For them, time is the continuous duration of the directly experienced. This latter interpretation eliminates all discontinuity, as well as all real movement or more precisely, all succession in time; it denies also any possibility of measuring or mastering time. From Aristotle I retain the idea that time is movement (rather a plurality of movements), and from his opponents the idea that time possesses a qualitative element, it is not always measurable and even more not always quantifiable.

JEAN PIAGET'S DEFINITION

The definition offered here does not depart much from the one Jean Piaget proposed in *Le développement de la notion de temps chez l'enfant*, (1946). Since his definition influenced me it would be useful to indicate how we differ. Piaget only speaks of "convergency", whereas I also insist on the "divergency" of *movements*. Piaget interprets convergency as an ordering of time, while I believe that "convergency" is first of all simply *correspondence*, and then perhaps also the coincidence of movements (simultaneity) but not parallelism, since there are multiple ways of succession. In opposing *intuitively grasped* time and *operative* time, Piaget considered the first related exclusively "to accomplished efforts and to felt changes", and the second, be it qualitative or on the contrary metric and quantitative, as always entirely *constructed* because it is linked to an "order of always reversible succession" (pp. 274–275). But I believe that Piaget has not sufficiently taken into account the *dialectic* between succession and duration, continuity and discontinuity, heterogeneous moments and homogeneity. He restricts the direct grasping of time and passes too quickly from "intuitive irreversibility" to the "operative reversibility" of time, thus destroying the intermediate degrees in which a large part of time moves. For these reasons he did not achieve an adequate grasp of the multiple manifestations of time. This derives from the fact that, according

19

to his own interpretation of his definitions, it is founded on a subjacent rationalist philosophy. I have tried to free my definition from this orientation as well as from all other philosophies.

IS MULTIPLE TIME POSSIBLE?

Perhaps, even granting the definition of time as a *convergency and divergency of movements which persist in a discontinuous succession and change in a continuity of heterogenous moments*, the question will be raised as to whether it suffices to make the multiple manifestations of time possible. Does this definition avoid the destruction of both real time and time concept? If there are multiple manifestations of time, if these are not integrated in one another and collide, so to speak, how can the world continue to exist? And why subordinate the multiple manifestations of time to the same time concept instead of coining other terms for each one? Were not thinkers as divergent as Aristotle, Kant and Hegel correct in insisting on the unity of time; a unity that Aristotle saw in *measure*, Kant in *transcendental form* of our sense intuition, and Hegel in the relation of *time* and *spirit*, always one and multiple at the same time (*Zeitgeist –Geist der Zeit*)?

Never has the intellectual atmosphere been as favorable to the awareness of the multiple manifestations of time as that of the twentieth century. Never before have the different manifestations of social time confronted each other as obviously as today. With the impressive development of communication technique, we pass in a twinkling through different manifestations and scales of time characteristic of various nations, types of societies, and groups. Both philosophy and the sciences reveal now that the asserted unity of time was a mirage. This is the consequence of the astonishing meeting of the Bergsonian philosophy of time and Einstein's general theory of relativity. For this reason we should digress for a moment to analyze the Bergsonian philosophy of time and the methodology of sciences today.

But before we can start, we must answer to the question of the possibility of the multiple manifestations of time and their unity. If time is either the divergency or convergency of movements, one can logically recognize as many manifestations of time as there are ways of the abovementioned convergencies and divergencies.

20

In principle, n + 1 times can exist; this is a question of the reality of facts and of the construction of facts by the operational conceptualization of the different sciences. All of these times in spite of their profound differences, possess the same formal characteristics of convergent or divergent movements, and thus enter into the general category of time.

As already noted, without attempts to unify the multiple manifestations of time into a hierarchized system, our personal life, social life, or orientation in the world are impossible. Such unifications are not given to us beforehand, but must be acquired through human effort in which a struggle for the mastery of time enters. We do not know and we shall never know if a unity of the multiple manifestations of time exists *in itself.* We can only struggle so that *we will not be lost in the multiple manifestations of time and in order to achieve a relative unification of the scales of time.* We are occupied with this problem, more or less successfully, in our psychic life, our social life, in our knowledge of time within and outside the sciences, in the physical sciences as well as in the social sciences.

BERGSON AND THE PROBLEM OF TIME

In order to clarify our position we shall stop a while for a detailed analysis of Bergson's theory of time. Bergson popularized the opposition of two times. The first of these is *heterogenous duration*, irreversible, "in becoming" (*"se faisant"*), characteristic of qualitative time belonging to that which he called "tension", particularly to non-automatic memory, to the *"élan vital"*, to creative freedom. The second time is *homogeneous succession*, reversible, accomplished time (*"tout fait"*), belonging to the "material world"; it is a quantitative time founded on spatialization. Although in *Matière et mémoire* and in *L'évolution créatrice* he discovered "different densities of duration" (*Matière et mémoire*, p. 273) and although he declared "that there is no unique rhythm" and that "one can easily imagine different rhythms, which are slower or more rapid, measuring the degree of tension or of relaxation of the consciousness and, by this, fixing their respective places in a series of beings" (*Matière et mémoire*, p. 231), and finally, although he placed matter, biological life, the psychic and the social, *in different degrees of qualitative time*, he did not successfully arrive at a theory of the multiplicity of time, which would appear to emerge from his own analyses.

21

There are many reasons for this unexpected stalemate: (a) First, Bergson, incorrectly, tied qualitative time to his *despatialization*. He, himself, had discovered in *Matière et mémoire* "concrete extensity", which is qualitative and thus different from quantitative space. It would appear to develop from this that "tension" and "extension" could be both quantitative or qualitative. He, however, continued to see in the different degrees of the density of duration, phases of despatialization. Furthermore, he continued to identify the conceptualizations of times and of extensities with their quantifications and their spatialization, thus over-simplifying the problems which he himself had foreseen. (b) Secondly, Bergson was a victim of his continuism. In spite of the fact that the *heterogeneous duration* of qualitative time appears loaded with *discontinuous* moments, Bergson never was able to render them actual. In Bergson's duration nothing begins and nothing ends. Also the degrees of density of the duration are included in such a continuity of passage that they do not separate nor oppose each other sufficiently. The lack of actual discontinuity interferes with recognition of multiple times. It is here that the constant threat of monism in Bergson arises, first psychological monism, then vitalistic and spiritualistic monism, and finally mystic-theological monism. In his last work, *Les deux sources de la morale et de la religion*, Bergson noted the stalemate of his attempts to unite in a single movement all the realities of the world unfolding in the qualitative duration. Then, in spite of his first inspiration to dethrone eternity in favor of human time, he was led to a new effort of reconciliation in "living eternity", reminiscent of Plotine and Augustine (c). Thirdly, Bergson was too insistent in his different works, sometimes on the present as an aspect of time (*Les données immédiates de la conscience*), sometimes on the past as dominant in time (*Matière et mémoire*), sometimes on the future as coloring time (worldly future in *L'évolution créatrice*, and on other-wordly future in *Les deux sources*). He was thus hindered from studying the varieties of possible combinations and different meanings of the present, past and future. Now, each of these aspects can dominate over the others or be projected in the others. The future can be rendered present and even past, the past projected into the future, the present rendered past and the past rendered present. This important variation contributing to the multiplication of times escaped Bergson. This is because, in spite of everything, he always used qualitative duration to develop previously accepted general philosophical theses having nothing to do with the analysis of time. (d) Finally, Bergson refused to admit that the "construct" of the sciences, that is their operational frames of reference, including their conceptualized time, measured and quantified up to a certain point, could be founded on experienced and grasped qualitative manifestations of time. The times of the different sciences appeared to him always opposed to qualitative duration and entirely spatialized. Thus Bergson cut the bridges between the multiplicity of times (which, in presenting discontinuism, he had discovered) and the plurality of times included in Einstein's theory of relativity, when he refused to admit that the constructed times of the sciences themselves carried the germs of the qualitative time. It is, moreover, interesting to note that both Gaston Bachelard, the scientific methodologist, and Jean Piaget, the psychologist, expressed amazement at the fact that Bergson never believed that he could learn something about time from Einstein's theory. He was struck by how intimately time and space were brought together in the multiple space-times and time-spaces of Einstein. To summarize the real reasons why Bergson, after having prepared the ground for the theory of the multiplicity of time, had not himself proceeded towards its development, was that he lacked the dialectic frame of mind. Nothing requires the dialectic approach more than the problem of *time*.

As a matter of fact, all the characteristics of time, always in degrees, can only be understood dialectically: the "discontinuous continuity" and the "continuous discontinuity", the duration in succession and the succession in duration, the past, the present and the future, sometimes projected in one another, sometimes dominant over one another, and finally sometimes reduced to one another, the "quantitative-qualitative" and the "qualitative-quantitative" (quantity itself presented in the form of degrees of extensity and intensity), the homogeneous heterogeneity, and the stable-change and the changing stability. Bachelard sensed it well, and entitled one of his books *La dialectique de la durée* (1936). If the procedure of dialectic hyper-empiricism (the complementarity, mutual implication, ambiguity, polarization and reciprocity of prespectives)[1] is applied to Bergson's discoveries, one arrives at the multiplicity of time directly.

---

[1] See G. Gurvitch, *Dialectique et sociologie*, 1962, pp. 189–220.

However, the Bergsonian endeavor still remains a very important anticipation of this.[1]

THE PROBLEM OF TIME IN CONTEMPORARY PHYSICS

Let us now see how Einstein's general theory of relativity and quantum physics have contributed to solving the problem of the multiplicity of time. Einstein demonstrated that in physics there are as many times as there are frames of reference and that the speed of movement is relative to the point of view of the observer who chooses one of these frames of reference. That is to say, among other things, that the time of macrophysics does not correspond to the time of microphysics, that the time of mechanics is not that of thermodynamics, nor the time of astronomy that of physics. But a too narrow connection between time and space, because it relates the frameworks of Time-Space and Space-Times, both quantified and continuous, did not allow Einstein to reveal that it is a matter not only of the difference of measures applied to the diverse times, but also of the qualitative differences and varied relations of past, present and future in these times.

Now quantum physics has drawn attention to this point. It has revealed, among other things, that the discontinuous radiations of electrons are produced in a time resistant to quantitative measures, time energy cut by intervals, of which even the rhythms are unfathomable. In these conditions the scientific theorists are led to speak of the "many times in physics which sustain various relations". This situation is best formulated in Bachelard's book *La dialectique de la durée* (1936): "If, until now, the physicist's time has appeared to be unique and absolute, it is because the physicist, first and foremost, was placed on a particular experimental plane. *Temporal pluralism has appeared with relativity. There are many times for relativity, to which, without doubt, it corresponds...*, but which do not keep absolute duration. *Duration is relative.* Nevertheless, in the doctrines of relativity the conception of duration still has continuity as an obvious characteristic. This is no more so in quantum physics. All the difficulties encountered in the assimilation of doctrines arise from the fact

[1] See my paper 'Deux aspects de la philosophie de Bergson – temps et liberté', *Revue de métaphysique et de morale* 1960, 307–316; and 'La théorie sociologique de Bergson', *La vocation actuelle de la sociologie*, Vol. II, 2nd ed., 1963, Chapter XI, pp. 203–219.

that a qualitative change is explained ... [by a] change in position. One can see that here continuity is .... a very poor hypothesis ... . It can then be presumed that quantum physics requires the conception of discontinuous durations which do not have the properties of chain reactions [d'enchâinements illustrées] ... by continuous trajectories" (pp. 90–91)

THE MULTIPLE MANIFESTATIONS OF TIME IN DIFFERENT SCIENCES

But if multiplicity of time forces itself on the natural sciences, how can we take exception to it in the social sciences where the conflicts of time are much sharper and much more striking? We must now answer the third question formulated in the second section of Chapter I: What does *Social Time* and *Multiple Social Time* mean? What is the specificity of these times? Do we admit specificity and multiplicity only of real social time of moving collectivities, or only of time constructed as operational frames of reference in sociology, or is it admitted also in time which can be, according to the situation, experienced, perceived, represented, symbolized and conceptualized, and also in time which can sometimes be quantified?

What is the meaning of time of inanimate nature, physical time, astronomical time, time of living nature, time of vegetable and animal life, time of species and organisms, time of the human body, psychic time and within it collective psychic time, intermental psychic time, individual psychic time, and again, psychic time of intellectual emotive or voluntary coloration. The spheres of reality which we can distinguish live in very different times, since the divergency and convergency of their movements are in correlation with the specificity of the first. The accentuations of present, future and past, of continuity and discontinuity, of duration and succession, of qualitative and quantitative, differ in all of them. In *physical reality*, the difference between present, past and future tends to be obliterated. In the *reality of stars* past and future obliterate the present. In *biological time* time is non-reversible and past, present and future oppose each other while augmenting discontinuity and the qualitative. In the *time of the human body* carrying the traces of psychic and social time, time is more discontinuous and more qualitative than all the other times mentioned up to now. Here abrupt changes of relations between present, past and future are sometimes manifested. In *psychic time*, already full of

25

meanings, the present is accentuated by breaking with the past and the future, etc... Thus, long before the different sciences began to construct their specific operational frameworks of time in which the object of their studies is placed, the multiplicity of time is forced on us by direct contact with the different spheres of reality. In the construction of time by different sciences as operational frameworks appropriate to their study, these initial tendencies of reality are brought into the open and conceptualized. From this point of view we can make the following observations:

(1) *Macrophysical* time does not correspond to *micro-physical time*, the first being time tied to the calculation of probability and large numbers, the closest approach to quantified succession, and the second being the time of radiations of electrons, whose relative continuity, if one can presuppose it, is only hypothetical.

(2) The time of *thermodynamics* does not correspond to time of *mechanics*, nor to the time of macrophysics. This time of the intensity of thermic phenomena, in raising the problem of their extinction, accentuates the future and the present more than the past, and reveals itself to be more qualitative than the time of mechanics.

(3) Time of *astronomy* cannot be reduced to any of the times constructed by physics. It is essentially a hypothetical time, tied to the quasi-infinite distance of light, where the present is obliterated, the past and the future alone remaining in play.

(4) The time of *chemistry* is different from the time of physics as well as of astronomy. The present is projected in the past and in the future and accentuates the passage from discontinuity to continuity and *vice versa*.

(5) In the time of *geological strata*, as stated by Michael Souriau in his book *Le temps* (1938, pp. 15–20) the past and the continuity, are emphasized but the qualitative is not sacrificed to the quantitative very much. It is like astronomical time in that it is a highly hypothetical time.

(6) *Biological time* (where botany time and zoology time can be distinguished) obviously cannot be reduced to any of the preceding times. Here it is a matter of cumulative time proceeding by leaps, time of evolution interrupted by discontinuities, vital time where the non-reversibility and the future proclaim their rights and where the qualitative begins to dominate. M. Lecomte de Nouy in his book *Le temps et la vie* (1936) is a protagonist of the specificity of this biological time. However, he did not distinguish between real time where vegetable and animal life abound, and

26

the time constructed by biology as a science. He was not yet ready to pay attention to the difference between biological time and the physiological time of the human body, as well as to time as reality and as it is constructed by physiology and anthropology.

(7) In this time, since it deals with the human body, not only is the biological side considered, but also the psychological and the sociological aspects. This is the time of changes of the human body and the time of the ages of man. Now, as Marcel Mauss has shown in his remarkable study, 'Les Techniques du Corps' (reprinted in *Sociologie et anthropologie*, 2nd ed., 1960, pp. 365–386,) some movements of the human body arise from society as do the techniques of breathing, walking, "manner of remaining upright", of reproduction, of eating, rowing, even of sleeping, etc... Man's life cycle is also very deeply penetrated by the social reality. His "ages" are socially defined and vary according to the type of global societies. The human and social meanings, penetrating into the time constructed by physiological anthropology, accentuates the ruptures between the past, present and future. Differentiation of ages and individual variation in longevity, and also the possibility of abrupt changes in these elements emerge from this discontinuity between past, present and future.

Time constructed by the *psychological* and *historical* sciences, as well as the time of historical reality itself will be discussed more fruitfully after our analysis of the time of social reality, and after dealing with the construction of time by sociology (see pp. 34 ff.).

SOCIAL TIME

Social Time is the time of convergency and divergency of movements of the *total social phenomena*, whether the *total social phenomena* are global, group or microsocial and whether or not they are expressed in the social structure. The total social phenomena both produce and are products of social time. They give birth to social time, move and unfold in it. Thus social time cannot be defined without defining the total social phenomenon.

The term "total social phenomenon" was coined by Marcel Mauss. He was inspired at first by a three-fold protest: against the decomposition of the social reality into separate elements; against a too static conception of social reality; and finally against the opposition between society and man

27

taken individually. "After having too much divided and abstracted, it is necessary" for the sociologist, Mauss wrote, "to reconstruct the whole in its irreducibility". The different social activities (religious, magical, technical, economic, cognitive, moral, juridical, political) can only be understood, as manifestations of a same whole which is the total social phenomenon. It would, at the same time, be extremely misleading to consider these phenomena in a congealed state, in "rigor mortis" [*cadaverique*] so to speak, according to the expression of Mauss. These turbulent forces are more "than the particular or the sum of institutions, more than all the organizations" and even more than all expressions of social reality in structures. The total social phenomena are the source of life and of social action, the "collectivities acting". Finally, and here Mauss agrees with Karl Marx, there is a tendency towards correspondence between total social phenomenon and total man. There is no economic man, political man, man as subject of law, as moral agent, *homo faber* and *homo sapiens*, one separated from the other. Man exists only as all of these and more besides. This "total man" cannot be reduced to his mental life not even to the collective consciousness. He is a body as much as he is a participant of societies, of classes of groups, of We-nesses: all representing total social phenomena. And by this reciprocal participation, the total social phenomenon participates in man as much as man participates in the whole. The tendency towards the correspondence, or better yet, towards the "reciprocity of perspectives", between the total social phenomenon and total man, is expressed by Mauss in the most obvious manner.[1]

In order to come closer to the total social phenomena, these actual always changing totalities of participation of the human in the human, it is indispensible to draw on points of reference, never indicated by Mauss. These consist in their depth levels on the one hand, and in their astructural, structurable, and structured elements on the other hand. The total social phenomena have an ontological primacy over all their depth levels, such as the ecological base, organizations, rites, procedures, practices, fashions, fads, patterns, social roles, collective attitudes, signs, signals, symbols, ideas, values, effervescences, collective mentality. From the exterior crust of the social – its ecological base (geographic, demographic,

---

[1] See on Mauss's conception of the "total social phenomenon" 'Introduction' to my *La vocation actuelle de la sociologie*, Vol. I, 3rd ed., 1963, pp. 15–24 and *Traité de sociologie*, Vol. II, 1960, pp. 333–338.

instrumental) passing through organizations, regular behavior, patterns, signs and symbols, to innovating collective behavior, to the collective ideas and values and to the mentality which grasps them intuitively or which creates them, the pulsation of total social phenomenon is manifested in a perpetual coming and going. All these levels permeating each other and struggling with each other are animated by the varied pulsations of continuity and discontinuity. Moreover, their accentuations change with each type of total social phenomenon, be it a *We*, a group, a class or a global society. Better yet, these accentuations, also change with conjunctures within the same structure. Peaceable, agitated, revolutionary, daily routine or special occasions (funerals, weddings, hunts, wars, internal or external struggles) influence these accentuations.

The interpenetrations and perpetual conflicts between these astructural, structurable and structured elements (the structures being multiple hierarchies in precarious balance) are accompanied by pitched battles between the spontaneous and organized elements of the social life. The social structures trying to utilize them, one against the others, are another point of reference for grasping the life of the total social phenomena. As a matter of fact, the total social phenomena, while subjacent to the web of all these elements and all these struggles, are never entirely expressed in any of them and always represent more than their interpenetration and evidently, more than their sum.

It is in the study of these divergencies, tensions, conflicts, antagonisms, as well as the complementarities, mutual implications and reciprocities of perspectives between the depth levels on the one hand, the structures and astructural elements on the other hand, that one becomes aware that the discontinuities and continuities between the levels of total social phenomena can only be studied with the dialectical approach. This is the only way to grasp the social totalities in their fluctuations and all the lacerations and participations belonging to them. If, after having found the total social phenomenon, Mauss did not conceptualize it with sufficient clarity, it might very well be because he had repudiated the dialectic. We maintain that the study of social time doubly calls for the dialectic, as neither the concept of time nor the social reality can be clarified without it.

In order to elaborate a more concrete notion of the specificity of social time, we shall try to delineate in our next section the different times which are met and which collide in the different depth levels of the total social

29

phenomena and in the opposition between the astructural, structurable and structured elements of these same phenomena.

Finally, social time is characterized by the maximum of human meaning which is grafted on it, and by its extreme complexity. Its complexity is much greater than that of the time of physical reality. Except for historic time, it is by far the most discontinuous of human times. Also, social time is more difficult to unify than all the other kinds of time. This leads to much variation in the hierarchies of social time manifestations and in the character of their consecutive interpenetrations.

VARIETIES OF SOCIAL TIME

We have defined Social Time as the *convergency* and *divergency of movements of the total social phenomena, giving birth to time and elapsing in time*. Specifically, the total social phenomenon is an actual total participation of the human in the human involved in an endless movement ebb and flow. The necessity for establishing a multi-dimensional perspective in order to grasp the total social phenomenon cannot be over-emphasized. In other words, the frame of reference must include the depth levels and the complicated play of astructural, structurable and structured elements. Social time, to which maximum human meaning is grafted, is extremely complex and full of the unexpected. We must try to arrive at a more concrete idea of social time in order to study the different manifestations of social time which collide and combine in the involvement of different levels, at the very heart of the total social phenomenon.

A sociological conceptualization of the multiple manifestations of social time must first be presented. The social manifestations of time are of so complex a character, in their variations and interpenetrations, that they cannot be described and studied without an operational framework, which only sociological theory can elaborate and present. This does not mean that sociology alone is qualified to study the spectrum of social time, which also presents an object of the other social sciences, particularly of historical knowledge. Whether it is a matter of real social time alone, or whether it is also the awareness of this time as it is grasped intuitively, perceived, symbolized, conceptualized, measured or mastered will not be prejudged. By *mastered*, is meant, as we already said the efforts displayed in certain structured social frameworks to rank the manifestations of time in a hierarchized scale. In any case, to analyze the real social time and the many ways of becoming aware and mastering it, a sociological conceptualization is needed.

In *Déterminismes sociaux et liberté humaine* (1955; 2nd revised ed., 1963) a general scheme of the kinds of social time was constructed in order to study the times corresponding to the different depth levels of social reality and to the different micro-social, group and all-inclusive total phenomena. This scheme mentioned in the Introduction is now presented in detail.

(1) *Enduring Time* (*time of slowed down long duration*). Here the past is projected in the present and in the future. This is the most continuous of the social times despite its retention of some proportion of the qualitative and the contingent penetrated with multiple meanings. For example, the ecological level moves in this time, particularly its demographic aspect. The past is relatively remote, yet it is dominant and projected into the present and the future: the latter thereby risks annihilation. It loses much of its concrete and qualitative coloration, and for this reason can be expressed in ordinary quantitative measures more easily than all other times. The quantitative measures, however, always remain inadequate. Kinship and locality groupings, especially the rural, are the particular groupings which tend to move in this time. Among the social classes it is the peasant class, and among the global societies the patriarchal structures appear to actualize this time.

(2) *Deceptive Time*. Under the guise of long and slowed down duration, it masks the virtuality of sudden and unexpected crises. In this "surprise time" a rupture between the past and the present occurs, reinforcing discontinuity. The organized level of social life unfolds in this time. This is a time of paradox, simultaneously slowed down and agitated. It is a time of long duration dissevered by abrupt crises and unforeseen explosions, interrupted by a flood of discontinuity. This time belongs also to large cities, and to passive communions, as well as to political "publics". Among the global societies, it is also the time (along with other times) of the *charismatic-theocratic* structures, which were meant to be everlasting, yet knew revolutions, as Ancient China and especially Egypt give evidence.

(3) *Erratic Time, time of irregular pulsation between the appearance and disappearance of rhythms* – an enigmatic series of intervals and moments

31

placed within duration. This is a time of uncertainty *par excellence* where contingency is accentuated, while the qualitative element and discontinuity become prominent eventually. The present appears to prevail over the past and the future, with which it sometimes finds it difficult to enter into relations. For example, it is the time of *social roles* and of *collective attitudes*, where regulated social roles collide with repressed, aspired, fluctuating and unexpected social roles. This is the time of the technical patterns, particularly in the societies of the nineteenth and twentieth centuries. In the micro-social sphere this is the time of mass sociability, especially of the passive mass sociability. This is also the time of non-structured groupings, such as are most of the non-political publics, and of the classes in the process of formation. This is the time of global societies in transition, as our society of today so often is.

(4) *Cyclical Time* in which an apparent precipitation masks a withdrawal into itself ("a dance on one spot"). The past, present and future are mutually projected into one another with an accentuation of continuity and a weakening of contingency, while the qualitative element is brought into sharp relief. This is often the time of communion sociabilities when they take on a mystic character. This time visibly prevails in the mystic-ecstatic groupings (churches, sects, mystic-ecstatic huts). It is predominant in the archaic societies where the mythological, religious and magical beliefs play such an important part. It is true, however, the magic, in-as-much as it competes with religion, overflows cyclical time.

(5) *Retarded Time* is a delayed time whose unfolding is awaited so long that, although the future is actualized in the present, it is not efficient. In this delayed time no equilibrium between continuity and discontinuity is attained. They tend to be equivalent, but the qualitative and contingent elements are reinforced. As examples, this is the time of the social symbols, always outmoded at the very moment when they are crystallized. Because they are awaited for so long, they often tend to be jaded very soon after they are expressed. Among the manifestations of sociability, it is community sociability which usually emphasizes retarded time. Community holds strongly its symbols and promotes jural regulations whose procedures preferably take place in delayed time. The groupings that move in retarded time are closed groupings or those to which admission is difficult: for example, the nobles, the landed gentry, certain corporations whose members are selected, particularly the licensed professions such as

academic faculties and more broadly public service professions. Among the global societies, it was the feudal society at the degree that feudal bonds predominated.

(6) *Alternating Time*, time alternating between delay and advance, where the realization of past and future compete in the present. Here discontinuity is stronger than continuity, without accentuation of the qualitative element and without enhancement of contingency. This is the time belonging to patterns, rules, signals, signs and collective conduct of some regularity. Here delay and advance struggle endlessly, as they are both of equal strength. The victory of one over the other can only end with a very bitter struggle and the issue is always precarious. This is often the time of communities when their tendency to immobility is shed. This is the time of the economic groupings, at least when other factors do not intervene to complicate matters. Finally, this time had first place in global societies at the inception of capitalism and when absolute monarchs ruled.

(7) *Time in advance of itself* or *time pushing forward* is a time where the discontinuity, contingency, and the qualitative triumph together over their opposites. The future becomes present. This is the time of collective effervescences, of aspirations toward the ideal and the common values, and of collective acts of decision and innovation. This is also the time of the active masses and communions in revolt. As a rule, it is the time of the proletarian class. This time was predominant in competitive capitalism, as has been indicated in my *Déterminismes sociaux et liberté humaine*.

(8) *Explosive Time* where the present as well as the past are dissolved in the creation of the immediately transcended future. In this time discontinuity, the contingent, and the qualitative are maximized and their opposites reduced to a minimum. This is the time of acts of collective creation, which, insofar as they are effervescent conduct, always intervene in social reality, but which, from a subjacent level, become apparent and dominant during revolutions. This is the time of creative Communion. In centralized and pluralistic collectivism there is an attempt to make this time dominant. In a more technicist form, there is at least a pretension toward having this time play a supporting role for organized capitalism and fascism. However, it is often so in appearence only, since it is only a matter of the time of the "sorcerer-apprentice". The explosive time, when it is effective, endangers the global and partial structures which move there, live dangerously and it involves maximum efforts.

33

SOCIOLOGICAL TIME AND HISTORICAL TIME

It is now desirable to clarify an important question we raised at the outset: the problem of knowing "how to distinguish social time studied by sociology from that studied by history". In other words, "is there a difference between sociological time and historical time?"

Here it is necessary to distinguish between the *reality* studied, the *method* applied to this study and the *object* which is the result of the marriage of the first two elements. To end the confusion between history as reality and historiography as science, it must be recognized that historical reality is a special part of social reality. Historical reality is the promethean collectively, in which the We-nesses, groups, classes, global societies become aware of themselves and of their ability to transform themselves and to modify the total social phenomena, especially the corresponding structures and organizations. Every total social phenomenon of global character, where the awareness of possible revolution or counter-revolution surges, as provoked by the collective will of the participants is an *historical society*. Historical reality, which exists outside of all historical method and all historiography, asserts and accentuates discontinuity because of its inherent prometheism.

But if we move from reality to method, we note a paradox. History as science applies a much more continuous method than does sociology. The method of sociology is typological, that of history is particularizing to the limit. The object of sociology is the typology of total social phenomena, types of micro-social elements, types of groupings, types of classes, types of global societies, and within most of them, types of movements of structuration and destructuration of total social phenomena. The latter are placed by sociology in *reconstituted* time according to their accentuated ruptures, that is to say, "in the process of being constituted and altered". The object of history is the promethean total social phenomenon in what it is not repeatable and replaceable. In its structure and below its structure it is placed in *reconstructed time* according to the criteria of a present given society, from the angle of a particular social class or of a specific group. In this reconstructed time the past is rendered present or the present is rendered past. From the methodological point of view, sociology is much more discontinuous than history as it is led to emphasize the discontinuity of types, scales and hierarchies of the

34

multiple manifestations of time. History, on the contrary, from the methodological standpoint, is led to fill in the ruptures and gaps, to throw up bridges between the social types, to pass without solution of the continuity from one global structure to another by linking together the movements of different global social phenomena which go beyond them. The historians do this in reconstructing the transition between total phenomena and thereby re-establishing the continuity of time.[1]

The paradox of continuity in the science of history which studies the historical reality inclining toward discontinuity, and of discontinuity in sociology which studies a more continuous social reality than that of history, is derived from three sources: (a) the ambiguity of historical time; (b) the total social phenomena invading and overthrowing the social structures and their types with volcanic impact; (c) the character of causality in history, unique at the same time it is closely-knit. Only the first point interests us here. I have already discussed this question in two writings; 'La crise de l'explication en sociologie' in *La vocation actuelle de la sociologie* (Vol. II, 2nd ed., 1963, Chapter XVI, pp. 462–481) and in my book *Dialectique et sociologie* (1962, pp. 224–232).[2]

In this last book, I developed my point of view most completely. In my former writings I reduced the ambiguity of historical time to the fact that it has already *elapsed*, is already *completed*, while sociological time is in the process of happening. I added that historical time is reconstructed according to the criteria of present societies and groups, which is the reason historians are driven to a constant rewriting of history, rendering historical time both more alive and more ideological. Finally the ambiguities of historical time lure it into "forecasting the past" and projecting this prediction into the future. I still maintain that these are necessary characteristics, but they do not suffice to explain the dialectic relations between the multiple manifestations of social time studied in sociology and in history, or more precisely, the dialectic between the multiplicity of sociological time and of historical time.

Historical reality as I have already noted is a circle inscribed within the

---

[1] See also my paper 'Continuité et discontinuité en histoire et en sociologie' in *Annales*, 1957, pp. 73–84.

[2] Thus it is necessary to distinguish the relative unification and interpenetration of the multiple manifestations of social time which sociology tries to study from the strong unification which historical science hopes to attain.

larger circle of social reality. The multiple manifestations of social time in historical reality are made prominent by their liaison with prometheism which emphasizes the alternating time of irregular pulsation of the time in advance beyond itself, and finally the time of creation. However, in historiography, actual historical time is reconstructed from the ideological point of view of the historian who is tempted to select certain of these times and exclude others. Then the manifestations of historiographical times do not correspond exactly to those of historical reality, but to those of the multiple reconstructions of the unfolding past by the historians. Now, the latter multiplicity, which is inevitable, is reduced to *multiple interpretations of the continuity of time*. Thus even at the core of historiography the two aspects of the multiplicity of time compete. This competition becomes far more dramatic than can be revived by the historians of the different societies and groups. They cannot succeed in reviving the unfolding time except at the price of projecting their own present into this time. They cannot realize this projection without supposing a continuity between the different scales of time belonging to these varied societies.

The fact that the historical method is individualizing, that it must emphasize the unique and unrepeatable character of the flow of events, leads to the reinforcement of the ties between cause and effect. It certainly helps the historian to underline the quasi-infinite particularities of historical time which are still much more varied than the time which is of sociological interest. But the time of historians specific as it may be, remains continuous, not only because it is projected and reconstructed, but because it assures the passages and transitions between the times of different structures and the times of various total social phenomena in perpetual movement.

Thus, the dialectical *ambiguity of historical time*, as well as its multiplicity is manifest everywhere:

(a) It is in the contradiction between the time of historical reality and the time which is projected by the historians.

(b) It is in the competition between the dual multiplicity of historical time: real multiplicity and interpreted multiplicity.

(c) It is in the opposition between their multiplicity, real and projected at the same time, and their continuity which is always taken for granted.

(d) It is in the individualizing and singularizing of historical time which only serves to reinforce their constructed continuity.

(e) It is in the fact that the time which has been unfolding, which is in a sense completed, has very few traits in common with time in the process of being made.

(f) Finally, it is even in the contact between historical time and sociological time. In spite of all their conflicts and tensions they need one another, they are dialectically complementary and often mutually imply each other.

The historians present their disagreements in the interpretation of historical time to the sociologists. They also remind the sociologists with discoveries of the particularly rich variations of historical time and their different unifications, that the continuous transitions between the global social phenomena of different types go beyond their structures. The sociologists provide the historians with points of reference for their particularizing analysis of discontinuous social time. They also help the historians take into account the ideological character of their own perspectives of time, revealing how necessary it is to limit the continuity between the scales of time. The sociologists explain why the historians are pushed to this continuism by their reconstructing, projecting and individualizing method.

The sociologists are much more broadminded than the historians. Recently Fernand Braudel claimed (cf. his study 'Histoire et Sociologie', *Traité de Sociologie* (Vol. I, 1958; 2nd ed., 1963), pp. 96–97) that only the historians are able to arrive simultaneously at the multiplicity and the unity of time "in the white, violent, unitary light" which is indispensible to the time of historians. Why? Because he believes that the historians alone possess the secret of surpassing "the narrowest issues of events" and have access to the "longest durations". Since no argument is advanced to support this thesis, if it is not an article of faith, it must be based on an assumption that historians alone are able to study the total social phenomena of global character, alone are able to show that these phenomena go beyond the structures, and finally alone have the ability to reveal the varying unifying interpenetrations of social time. However, as we have already implied and will bring into concrete, sharp focus in a later chapter[1], all these presuppositions only give evidence of an imperialistic frame of mind inclined to favor historical science over sociology

[1] Cf. Chapter VII, devoted to Global Societies and their Time Scales.

and to ignore the dialectic between both. We can only take cognizance of this frame of mind, regret it, and hope that it will be reappraised so that true co-operation can be established between sociology and history to study the multiplicity and varied unifications of social time.

38

CHAPTER III

THE DEPTH LEVELS AND SOCIAL TIME

In order to develop a more concrete idea of the specific character of social time manifestations, we must first attempt to describe the different kinds of time which meet and clash in relation to the pluri-dimensionality of the total social phenomena and their corresponding structures.

Utilizing the scheme of the eight kinds of time which were outlined in the second chapter, we shall now attempt to characterize the time corresponding to each depth level. Obviously it will be more a matter of real social time than of awareness of time or mastery of time. We have already tried to show in several books the necessity (mentioned in the Introduction and in Chapter II) for a depth sociology which takes into account the many strata of social reality and arranges them into a multiplicity of levels. This is the one way of successfully achieving a frame of reference indispensible for grasping total social phenomena of all types. If then, social time is convergency and divergency of movements in the total social phenomena, it is first manifested as time of the plurality of dimensions, or in other words, of the different depth levels.

We shall begin with the time where the ecological surface tends to move and then deal with the other depth levels. However, we shall first answer some objections that may possibly be raised: (a) No ulterior philosophical motive nor value judgement should be supposed. The terms "supra" and "infra", "superposed" and "subjacent", "more superficial" and "more profound" mean only "what appears more or less directly accessible" to our perception, to our knowledge, or to our intuition. (b) Whether the accentuation of levels, their importance and their strength varies in the different total social phenomena *is a question of fact and of fact only*. Only experience can establish how the flexible interpenetration of levels varies in relation to different social frameworks, to their structures and conjunctures. (c) There is a question as to whether a single dimension or a single level and its corresponding time ever arises in social reality, and whether dividing social time is valid. For us all the moving levels fundamentally permeate one another, and yet they enter into tension, conflict and perpetual divergency. The strength of their continuity and discontinuity, of their complementarity, of their mutual involvement, of their symmetry and their polarization is to be studied anew in each case. And this is equally true for the social time in which they move and which never remains isolated.

ECOLOGICAL TIME

This social time corresponds to the external environment, natural as well as technical, to objects, bodies, subjects and their behavioral participation in social life which can be grasped in the perception of the environment. The demographic and geographic aspect of the total social phenomena belongs to this domain; the density of the population, its distribution in relation to the soil, its migration from country to city and *vice versa*, the attraction exercised over it by the different regions or different urban neighborhoods, the social center or habitat of groups, the soil and territories of communes and parishes, provinces, departments, States, etc... belong to this domain. Also included are the monuments, buildings, churches, barracks, prisons, cottages, huts, factories, stores, the different thoroughfares, as well as the varied vehicles, tools, instruments, machines, industrial and agricultural products, foodstuffs, etc. More than all the other levels of social reality, the ecological surface can be adequately expressed in numbers, equations, graphs, and statistics. Does not the exterior world appear to unfold in a time close at hand and where the problem of measurement and of quantification is easily solved?

However, one must not forget that the movements of the ecological base are deeply penetrated and transfigured by collective human action. The soil and the natural milieu are fundamentally modified by techniques, attitudes, collective conduct and beliefs which fashion them. Population increase and decrease, density, migrations are in functional relationship with particular social organizations, specific structures, practices, regulations, symbols, ideas, values, collective mentality. For example, the deeper levels can exercise a direct influence on human fertility. The birth rate is higher among the faithful of certain religions which consider birth control a sin, than it is among the believers for whom obedience does not include such a prohibition. It must not be forgotten, that the "style of life", traditions, customs, practices, fashions, ideologies all intervene in demo-

40

graphic change. Finally, the conscious policy of governments interested in the density population also exercises considerable influence here.

This relationship with the other depth levels is still more evident for other material manifestations of social reality. For example, houses, thoroughfares, tools, instruments, machines, etc... could not have been invented, utilized, adapted or handled without the intervention of the other depth levels, which permitted them, favored them, or needed them. The technical patterns are inseparably tied to the cultural patterns but they can also enter into an endless conflict with the latter. Thus atomic energy and inter-planetary satellites threaten to overwhelm social structures and civilizations.

Essentially the time of the total social phenomena reverberates in the ecological level as the latter strains between the migration of population and technological change, sometimes convergent, sometimes divergent. But while the ecological level cannot be detached nor isolated from the total social phenomena, the time of the ecological surface tends to manifest certain characteristics which are specific to it.

We have already cited the time of this level as an example of enduring time of slowed down, long duration, the past prevailing over the present and the future, emphasizing continuity more than discontinuity. As a matter of fact, ecological time narrows the present to the utmost and seeks the most direct passage of the past into the future and thus is most attractive to the zealots of quantification or even of sociological naturalism. However, both are always forced to restrain themselves, by recognition of qualitative elements. Other unidimensional social times intervene here, as for example, those where the technical and cultural patterns, moral and juridical regulations, social roles and collective attitudes, symbols, collective ideas and values move. These are erratic time, time alternating between advance and delay, conquering advance and including explosive time itself. These times erupt in enduring time of slowed down, long duration. They make the present prevail, reverse the demographic forecast, revolutionize the technical tools, and completely modify natural resources. Not only wars and revolutions, but also technical inventions and changes of beliefs produce these effects. To this must be added the always existing possibility of a sharp rupture between ecological time and that of the other depth levels, as for example, in the lack of workers in the New World Colonies; or the rupture of the continuity of generations

41

experienced in France after the war of 1914–1918 and in Russia after the war of 1941–1945.

Finally, let us note that the awareness of ecological time once again introduces discontinuity and advance in this time which is presumed to be of long duration and slow motion. So does the manner of grasping it intuitively, conceptualizing it, symbolizing it, measuring it, as well as the effort to master it in submitting it to human control. Examples of the latter are prolonging the life of man, creating artificial lakes, and planning the combination of technical tools and the distribution of population. The human meanings with which this level is penetrated are apt to alter its course and reinforce the ruptures in continuity.

TIME CHARACTERISTIC OF ORGANIZATIONS

Organizations are a combination of collective, pre-established conducts which are arranged beforehand, hierarchized, and centralized according to certain patterns. These patterns are reflected on and fixed in advance in more or less rigid schemes usually formulated in the statutes. It is this organized level which, in the narrow sense of the term, exercises "constraints" over the participants and even over the non-participants. Moreover, it imposes the same constraints over the more spontaneous levels of social reality which always rest subjacent to it, beginning with the structures because they are not adequately incarnated or expressed in organizations. This is so because the structures are infinitely richer, full of nuances, and more flexible than organizations.

The organized level is usually more mobile and more dynamic than the ecological level, but often more ponderous and more formalized than the less crystallized levels of social life, including the patterns, signs, customs and fads. Organization serves as a catalyst to social spontaneity with which it is in dialectical relation. This is so because in spite of its inclination to check social spontaneity, the organization needs the invigorating force of the last. The degrees of immobility, rigidity, and social distance that an organization manifests do not depend on its arrangement alone, but also on the intensity of the subjacent levels.

This is true also for the social structures in which the organizations are integrated. As a matter of fact the organizations are part of the precarious balance of multiple hierarchies which make up a social structure. But the opposite is never possible. Social structure can never be integrated into organization, because the structure is pluri-dimensional, while the organization is unidimensional. Organization is always one of the subordinated elements of a structure which, where its exists, is infinitely more complex than its expression in one or more organizations. Thus, among the different types of structure one can distinguish those in which organization plays an important role (as in contemporary global structures) and types of structures in which the role of organization is much less important (for example, in the structure of early competitive capitalism). At the same time, if "structure" and "organization" are considered according to their general tendencies, structures are much more dynamic and mobile than organizations. This is because structures are involved in a perpetual movement of structuration, destructuration, and restructuration, while organizations are more rigid, crystallized, and immobilized because they are dominated by schemes arrested prematurely in the organizational statutes. However, everything finally depends on the type of social structure and the total social phenomenon which is subjacent to it. Sometimes these render the organizations more explosive and more active than the structures. (This is the case in our present situation). Sometimes they render the organizations more ponderous, rigid and slower than the structures. (This is the case in most of the primitive and feudal organizations, the ancient regimes, etc...).

This preliminary description of the organized level of social reality gives us an inkling that the social time in which it unfolds is not univocal and presents a special complexity. The time of organization is an example of deceptive time, "time of surprise", time slowed down but pierced by sharp crises and unforeseen explosions. Here continuity and discontinuity collide and never achieve an effective compromise. Erratic time, enduring time, time alternating between advance and delay, and explosive time meet here and permeate each other. The pre-established arrangements, already fixed in the statutes of an organization, obstruct innovating action of the participants, while favoring the action of the leaders who are themselves limited in their initiative. However, in order for the organization to endure or survive, it must adapt to new situations rather than fossilize and be shattered by excessive rigidity. To accomplish this, the organized level cannot turn inward too much on itself. It must free itself as much as possible from the domination of the past over the present and future. The solution closest to continuity is innovation through practices which soften the regulations and end by modifying them. Thus the time alternating between advance and delay intervenes in the life or organizations. But it is often revealed to be very inadequate. Important decisions are sometimes thrust on the organization which require direct action not covered by the statues or are contrary to them, or which, in certain cases, involve a sudden change of the statutes. Then it is apparent that organizations are directed by men, and that they risk being smashed because of inertia as well as because of incorrect maneuvers. This is why the time of organizations, in which delay and continuity appear to prevail, hides a virtuality of reinforced discontinuity and ruptures between the present and past. Better yet: the slowing down and delay are only possible here if the more or less long intervals are sometimes interrupted by a flood of discontinuity, advance and even of explosions. Thus, this time belongs to the "deceptive time" or "time of surprise". However, its intensity and effectiveness varies according to the structures and conjunctures.

The awareness of the time in organizations differs according to whether it is a matter of leadership, participants who benefit, conformists, or participants in revolt. The time is always too short for the first and too long for the last. Also leaders try to master the time in order to prolong it, while the participants in revolt try to master the time in order to shorten it, and provoke to overthrow of the organization. The success of these divergent tendencies depends on the situation in the structures and the total social phenomena.

THE TIME OF CONDUCT OF SOME REGULARITY OF PATTERNS, OF RULES, OF SIGNALS AND SIGNS

This covers a vast domain. It includes the inciting images, criteria, stimulants, substitute expressions, signals, signs destined to direct not only collective and individual conduct, but also roles and attitudes and finally mental life itself. It overflows the organized level and is realized in the more or less regular collective conduct manifested not only outside of all organizations, but sometimes even independently of a precise structure. The manifestations of this level start from the rather rigid ritual and procedural conduct to more fluid practices, mores, ways of life, and reach the entirely flexible spheres of fashions and every changing fads. Borderline cases are the deviant, erratic, non-conforming, resisting collective conduct whose importance should not be underestimated.

The patterns, rules, signals, signs are guides, directives, prescriptions or sometimes norms, which claim validity and require obedience, often even compel it. They act as effective determining forces of social reality of which they are both products and producers. Furthermore, they are only effective in the social reality of which they are parts when they are recognized as valid prescriptions or norms. The prescriptive and the determinative coincide here, what sometimes reinforces rather than loosens the obstacles represented by traditional or standardized patterns and orderly conduct in their opposition to movement and change. In other cases the patterns and rules are manifesting their capacity of innovation. Moreover, there are ruptures and an hiatus between the patterns and the conduct which realize them, as well as competition and conflict often surge up between patterns, rules, and different signals which cancel each other out.

This ambiguous and multivalent atmosphere of the patterns, rules, signs and fairly regular conduct have repercussions over the time which they produce and in which they evolve. *This is a time in which delay and advance try to engage in an endless struggle which is resolved in alternation.* Thus alternating time is highlighted here. As a matter of fact, in regard to delay, when rules and patterns are customary they can arise from a much more distant past than the statutes of an organization. But conversely, they can also be of a very recent date, representing the "last word", the latest discovery, the most recent issue, facing the future much more than the present and *a fortiori* much more than the past. It is a matter then, of definite leaps ahead not only in the technical or economic domain, but also in the juridical, moral, aesthetic domain. One only has to call to mind the struggle between the patterns and rules of the past and those of the future in Southern United States when the slaves were freed, in Japan since the inception of capitalism, and in postrevolutionary France, Russia and China.

Special attention must be paid to the fact that patterns and rules are sometimes oriented toward routine immobility, sometimes towards flexibility, and adjustment to circumstances and sometimes toward innovating initiatives. One comes to the conclusion that time leaping forward and retarded time are here both equally accentuated. They are equal in force, and always risk neutralizing each other. For this reason the

45

only possible solution is the time alternating between delay and advance. Victory of one over the other requires a persistent struggle, always with essentially precarious results. In this time manifestation, continuity and discontinuity, whether qualitative or quantitative, yield nothing to one another. This is also the case for the past and the future, both of which battle for their realization in the present.

TIME OF SOCIAL ROLES AND COLLECTIVE ATTITUDES

Social roles are a network of spring-boards for possible collective and individual action. They contribute to the structuration and the destructuration of social frameworks, sometimes only in realizing the expected, sometimes innovating or even modifying more or less profoundly, and in extreme cases, contributing to the re-creation of social frameworks and their structures. The depth level of social roles, which combine and interpenetrate, seems to be more spontaneous than that of the conduct of different degrees of regularity and patterns. It is true that certain social roles which are imposed on conduct at first glance appear to serve as important reference points for regularity, regulation, structure and indeed of organization. However, on closer examination, one realizes that these roles penetrate below the cristallized surface in the spontaneous reactions. Spontaneous reactions make the roles, whether collective or individual, overcome all patterns, all prescriptions, all social regularity and as a result, all standardization. As a matter of fact, the interpenetration, realization, and concrete combination of roles played by groups, by collectivities, and by individuals in a particular conjuncture contain the greatest surprises and leave considerable margin for unexpected attitudes, not only those which had been repressed, but sometimes those which are directly innovating and creative. Moreover, the self, we-nesses, groups, classes, and global societies play multiple social roles, sometimes more or less foreseen, sometimes unforeseen and even unforeseeable. Furthermore, a whole array of social roles can be established. Thus among the more or less foreseen or at least foreseeable roles, one can distinguish the privileged roles, organized roles, assigned roles, ordered roles, customary roles, virtual roles and the roles to which one only aspires. Among the unpredictable roles can be distinguished the fluctuating roles, the unexpected roles, the invented roles and the created roles. The social roles are never expressed entirely in behaviour, and sometimes they are not expressed there at all. This is because interpretation by the role holders is dynamic and their realization involves a subjacent element. The *collective attitudes* constitute this subjacent level.

Attitudes can never be reduced to the mental only; it is a matter of the imponderables of a social atmosphere, of a whole configuration that is more than its composing elements. Attitudes can be provisionally described as the *dispositions which push the we-nesses, selfs, groups, classes, entire societies to act and react in a certain way, to assume particular social roles.* Certainly, it is possible that these dispositions never materialize or only partially materialize. But even when they remain only in a virtual state, they arise from the total social phenomenon. Attitudes are a component element in the formation of all groupings and serve as a base for the roles as well as symbols and values. They can be defined as collective configurations, more virtual than actual, which involve the tendencies of the collectivities or of their members to assume particular social roles. They also constitute the social frameworks where specific values are sometimes accepted, sometimes repudiated or where pre-dispositions to certain preferences and dislikes, to certain conducts and reactions to them are manifested. Ordinarily, collective attitudes appear more continuous than they are in reality. Occasionally they can be very persistent, but they are often very fluid. They can also explode, reverse, or disclose abysses that are subjacent to them. In any case they always give an inkling of the more spontaneous levels of social reality.

The great variety of social roles and their active dynamism, as well as the multi-valence of collective attitudes and their enigmatic opacities, make discontinuity predominant over continuity, the unforeseeable over the foreseeable, the qualitative over the quantitative. Ruptures and discontinuities are multiple and intense here. There are ruptures and discontinuities between the very different, if not conflicting, social roles that individuals and groups play in various social and political conjunctures. An example is the radical change of the revolutionary, moderate, conservative and reactionary roles of groups and classes as the situation changes. There are ruptures and discontinuities in the different attitudes assumed by the same individuals and groups in different circumstances such as strikes, wars, revolutions, disasters, periods of prosperity, of stagnation and economic crisis. There are ruptures between social roles and

collective attitudes when these ostensibly overturn the hierarchy of anti-
cipated roles and propel towards the creation of new roles, or when the
social roles conflict with superannuated attitudes or attitudes which are
not appropriate to the circumstances. There are ruptures and discontinuities between the roles and attitudes of classes, groups and different
individuals which are antagonistic or in temporary conflict, going through
aggravated or moderated phases.

The social time produced by the very complex and upset level of
roles and attitudes carry traces of these immanent and constant jolts. It is
a time of uncertainty *par excellence*; uncertainty in the relationship between the present, past and future; uncertainty in the victory of discontinuity or continuity; uncertainty in delay or advance. Contingency triumphs
here. The time of this level is an erratic time of irregular pulsation, of
unpredictable fluctuations between the appearance and disappearance of
rhythms. Besides, the different rhythms compete, sometimes combining,
sometimes in mutual self-destruction. This erratic time tends to wed its uncertain flow to other kinds of time from which it seems to seek support.

The regular social roles appear to favor the time of patterns and
rules, that is the time alternating between delay and advance. In contrast,
the virtual roles or aspired roles which are fluctuating, unexpected, and
created, seem to move in time leaping forward where the future is effectively present, or even in explosive time where both the present and the
past dissolve in the creation of the future. However, it cannot be forgotten
that in erratic time of irregular pulsation, the present sweeps away the
future just as it does the past to which it does not always easily relate.

Often the collective attitudes evolve in an enduring time which appears
to be of long duration and slowed down or at least in a delayed time. This
does not always hinder the attitudes from occasionally being shaken with a
staggering force, either to be submerged, or to be completely reoriented.
Moreover, the times of arhythmic fluctuations, explosion and forward
thrust do not always succeed in clearing a path toward the future. This is
because they are due not only to the predominance of certain roles and
the disturbance of certain attitudes, but also to the performance and interpretation of each role as it is played, as well as the uncertainty of even
the most firmly established attitudes.

Thus social roles and attitudes unfold in a time in which continuity and
slowing down is insecure and combines a strongly accentuated contingen-

cy with discontinuity. This uncertain time is full of unexpected seething and pent-up fire but does not always successfully find a way for the present to move toward the future. Hence, roles and attitudes move in "deceptive time", cyclical time, and time leaping forward. One could say that in the erratic time of roles and attitudes, the predominant present, the uncertain past and future shift unceasingly in an interminable three-step.

TIME OF SYMBOLS, IDEAS AND COLLECTIVE VALUES

Social symbols are signs which only partially express the contents toward which they are oriented. They serve as mediators between these contents and the collective and individual agents who formulate them and to whom they are addressed. This mediation consists of encouraging the participation of agents in the symbolized contents and these contents in the agents. Whether the symbols are mainly intellectual, emotional, or voluntary, whether they are tied to the mystic or the rational, one of their essential characteristics is that *they reveal while veiling and veil while revealing, and even while they encourage participation, they check it.* From this viewpoint, all the symbols, including the sexual symbols, constitute a way of overcoming and dealing with obstacles and impediments to expression and to participation. The symbols vary because of many factors; particularly because of the character of the subject-broadcasters and the subject-receivers, because of the variable importance of the symbols and that what is symbolized; because of the various degrees of their crystallization and flexibility, etc. This is why the symbols constantly risk being overwhelmed, of being slower than that which they would symbolize. Only rarely are they adjusted for their task, so much so that at each turn we are tempted to speak of their "fatigue", if not of their "defeat".

In one sense, all the levels of social reality can be considered as symbols. But what in fact do the different levels of social reality symbolize? In the first place, the whole of a social reality which cannot be broken up. The levels of the total social phenomena, whether they interpenetrate or are in conflict (ordinarily they are both at the same time), are inadequate mediators (that is to say, symbols). In the second place, symbols, the products and producers of social reality, function as a kind of fluid and always present social cement, which infiltrates between the levels and continously cements their always new fissures and divergencies.

But if the social symbols symbolize above all the undissolvable whole of the levels, at the same time they are attached more specifically to the cultural products, to ideas and to collective values to which they can only give inadequate expression. The cultural products, including language, knowledge, morality, art, religion, law, and the ideas and values which they involve, are in a special relation to the symbols. The sphere of ideas and of collective values is their direct subjacent level. The symbols express ideas and values and serve as vehicles of participation in them; moreover, they contribute to the ideological justifications of the mentioned. But the fact that sociology is concerned with the level of collective ideas and values, does not mean that sociology has to solve philosophical problems. Sociology does not have to affirm the objective validity of values and ideas, nor to unmask their character of projection or epiphenomena. When the sociologist meets ideas and values acting in social reality, he does not have to do anything but state a fact and a fact only. A certain number of ideas and values cannot be lived, grasped, experienced, known, without the intervention of collective as well as individual intuitions and judgements. As soon as a collectivity becomes aware of them, they are already placed in sociological perspective; that is to say that their frames of reference are sociologically delimited or, in other words, that the social frameworks coincide with the cognitive and estimative frames of reference.

The spheres of symbols, ideas and values is even more discontinuous than that of the social roles and attitudes. There is a true hiatus here between symbols and that which is symbolized, between the different symbols, with an almost infinite variety of color, origin and effectiveness. There is discontinuity between ideas and values, between different ideas, ruptures between the accepted ideas and new ideas, discontinuity between the different hierarchies of values and between different values.

However, all this does not decide about the intensity in the dynamism of symbols, ideas and values. As a rule, the intellectual symbols are slower moving than the ideas, while the values, and particularly the willed values move faster than the ideas. Affective values are either behind or ahead of the ideas. The ideas intended to guide the collectivities are very often immobilized too quickly. They then demand a passive obedience, and impede movement while pretending to be evident, necessary, and eternal. In the form of "accepted ideas" they press for a delay. The willed and active collective values can themselves mark the stopping point, harmonizing too easily among themselves, becoming too dependent on accepted ideas and intellectual symbols, petrified and embodied in fixed situations, pretending to be eternal, posing as predestination, destiny, perfection. They then become the supporters of delay. When they are tied to affective values, aesthetic and particularly religious values, the ideas push easily towards the cyclical time of an apparent precipitation which covers a mobile "dancing around the bush" of the we-nesses, groups, and societies (thus provoking the illusion of "living eternity").

Taking these statements into account, we can say that the symbols, ideas and collective values unfold in a time in which delay and advance struggle, but never achieve alternation nor compromise. The intellectual ideas, and *a fortiori*, their symbols, normally tend to endure to an excessive degree and to move in a time held back on itself. That means that the symbols are often outmoded at the very moment when they crystallize; they are overworked and used up more or less rapidly. Most of the new ideas are awaited too long a time and by the time they are clarified they are not always "of their time". The future, which the ideas seek to actualize in the present without always rendering this future effective, is often no longer a future at the moment when the ideas are finally accepted. However, the ideas and even their symbols can in some cases also unfold in a time in advance of itself which renders the future effectively present. Such are the moments of discovery of new ideas, in the epochs of reform, renaissance, and revolution, or in the decisive moments when civilizations interpenetrate. This is also what happens when symbols participate in the creation of what is symbolized, as we can observe in the sciences; for instance in contemporary quantum physics.

Values linked with affectivity, the aesthetic, vital, erotic values tend to move in a time that is sometimes in advance and sometimes held back on itself. Sometimes these values unfold too quickly to be effective, sometimes they endure too long and end by becoming uncertain.

The willed values and symbols tied to morality sometimes succeed in being ahead of themselves. The moral values then precipitate their time foreward toward the explosive time of creation which they try to join. Here the past and the present are taken over in the future. But alas! It is for a very short, too short an instant, because the explosive time of creation is the least durable of all time manifestations.

51

COLLECTIVE MENTALITY AND TIME

We shall confine ourselves to a short statement about collective mentality and its time. Inasmuch as collective mentality is a matter of collective mental *states*, collective *opinions* and finally collective *acts*, it is placed in functional correlation with social situations, conjunctures, structures and total phenomena, the entire array of social time is found here, differently accentuated, combined and interpenetrated. Only in grasping it, perceiving it, trying to represent and conceptualize it, does the collective mentality become aware of its time.

In studying the dimensional plurality of social time associated with the depth levels, we never intended to separate the levels, one from the other, nor from their total social phenomena. We only wished to unveil a picture of the complexity of social time and show how the different manifestations of time meet, enter into conflict, are combined, and finally interpenetrate each other. In the partial social structures, and above all in the global social structures, the levels and their corresponding time begin to be arranged in apparent, fixed hierarchical scales where they permeate each other in a specific fashion. There, in the macro-sociological domain of structures, the problem of the mastery and relative unification of time by collectivities is clearly posed.

CHAPTER IV

THE MICRO-SOCIAL FRAMEWORK AND ITS TIME: THE MANIFESTATIONS OF SOCIABILITY

Manifestations of sociability are the many ways of being bound to the whole and within the whole. This is the micro-social scale of total social phenomena. Most of the different levels of social reality and the social time belonging to these levels can be actualized in manifestations of sociability since they are also total social phenomena. This includes not only the most spontaneous levels of mental states, acts, ideas, values, innovating behavior, attitudes and aspired social roles, but also the less spontaneous levels of patterns, rules, practices and finally of the ecological base. Micro-social elements, because of their infinite flexibility, embody in their incessant fluctuations the most uncertain aspects of social time manifestations and of the rather unseizable passages between them.

Are the micro-social manifestations of social time possible? Is it fruitful to be concerned with them? We do agree that in different sociabilities, fluctuations and uncertainty block the arrangement of depth levels and their social time manifestations into balanced hierarchized scales. The fluctuations and uncertainty also limit the spontaneous promotion of precise kinds of time. This seems to be reinforced because the micro-social elements deviate and change according to the different groups, structures, classes and global societies in which they are included. For example, different social times are produced by mass sociability actualized in the charismatic societies, in the Roman Empires, in the capitalistic, and in the collectivistic regimes.

But if all these limitations are rigorously exact, they would not at all stop the inquiry into the tendencies revealed by the manifestations of sociability, insofar as they unfold in specific social time. For if these social times possess less precise contours than the social time of groups, classes and global societies, if they cannot be hierarchized, and if they can be influenced by the time of the real collective units into which they are integrated, they in their turn, complicate and alter the social time of these collective units. It is a matter here of a complex dialectic between the time of the manifestations of sociability, the time of groups and classes and the time of global societies. Thus, in order not to mislead, no point of reference of the social time of the we-ness and of the relations with others can be neglected. If, for example, the sociability of widely dispersed masses, which evolves in erratic time intervenes in charismatic societies where cyclical time predominates (a time of apparent precipitation which covers a dance around the bush), the scale of time is modified. Likewise, the intervention of the community time (which is largely delayed time), in the time of proletarian classes (which tends to be in advance and precipitous, rendering the future present) complicates the time where the life of the proletarian social classes unfolds. One can thus, correctly, study social time where the micro-social frameworks tend to move without losing sight of the fact that only a single variation of the total situation is being taken into consideration.

Furthermore, another doubt can be expressed and the question raised as to whether the social time of the manifestations of sociability, so uncertain and so fluctuating, are not less easily grasped than the others because it is only a matter of lived and experienced real time, but not of the clear consciousness of time (perception, conceptualization, symbolization) and still less a matter of the mastery of time. Now, this reservation appears to be justified only with the acknowledgement that the time in which the manifestations of sociability unfold are not *always* accompanied by a consciousness of time and *a fortiori* by an effort to master it. However, we are going to see precisely that certain manifestations of sociability, in certain circumstances, do have these tendencies and that it will be essential to show it in each case.

In many of my writings I have tried to paint a picture of the microcosms of sociability manifestations which, in different degrees of actuality and virtuality can be discovered in the interior of each group, and indeed, in each global society. This leads us to indicate here the character of those micro-social elements which are particularly salient and convenient as points of reference for our analysis of the time.

Thus in the sociability of partial fusion in a we-ness, and in the sociability of partial opposition to others, we only choose the three degrees of intensity of the we-ness, Mass, Community and Communion, and the three degrees of relations with others, the relations of approach, the mixed relations, and the relations of withdrawal. Again, among these relations we will only take into consideration those which are established among the we-ness, groups and global societies, disregarding the quasi-infinite temporalities of interpersonal relations, which have so many variations that it would be tedious to dwell on all of them. As we are going to try to show, these six manifestations of sociability move in different social times, and the characteristics of these social times vary again when the contrast between passive sociability and active sociability is taken into account. Moreover, among these twelve micro-social frameworks some do and others do not have the capacity to lead towards the awareness of the time that they produce. Also, they have an unequal ability to master time.

Let us begin with *Mass, Community* and *Communion*. We mean by Mass the minimum degree of intensity of participation in the we-ness, accompanied by the strongest *pressure*. The whole exercises the weakest *attraction* ever the participants. This makes possible an almost unlimited expansion of size. *Community* has a medium degree of intensity of participation in the we-ness, medium pressure and also a medium attraction of the whole over the participants. *Communion* has a maximum degree of intensity of participation in the we-ness and exercises a minimum degree of pressure over its members. The size tends to contract in order to maintain the force and the depth of the fusion.

We call Mass, Community, Communion and more broadly all manifestations of sociability *passive* when they do not intend to accomplish collective works. The emotional coloration of attitudes and conducts involved here, predominates over will and the various intellections which accompany it. Active Mass, Community, Communion and manifestations of sociability are those which intend to carry out collective tasks. The voluntary coloration of the mentality, attitudes, and conducts involved here predominates over emotion and intellection which accompanies it. Passive sociability is carried to the extreme when it descends into the subconscious and the unconscious. Inversely, active sociability attains its highest degree when the will predominates in action and above all in mental acts of volition such as choice, decision and creation.

Mass, Community and Communion are *not* groups, but are *degrees* of partial fusion in the we-ness. Since these degrees belonging to the micro-social are often confused with the groupings, the following clarifications are offered in order to establish this distinction:

(a) *The intensity of the fusion in the We-ness and the pressure felt by its members, far from being positively correlated as one would think, are in inverse proportion.* As a matter of fact, it is precisely in the case where the fusion and participation in the we-ness remains at the surface and is not integrated in the most intimate levels of the self and others (that is in the Mass) that the pressure of the whole over its members is revealed to be strongest. Conversely, the more the partial fusion comes to include the personal depths and to make the individual members participate in the we-ness, the less the pressure of the whole over the Self and Others is felt. It is weaker in Community than in Mass; it is weakest in Communion, to such a point that it is scarcely felt at all. Thus when a we-ness contracts and intensifies into Communion, the self and others have the sensation of being increasingly freed from pressure. If the same we-ness is slackened into the Mass, its members have a sensation of increased pressure.

(b) *The intensity and the volume of the partial fusion in the We-ness are not positively correlated. They are again in inverse proportion.* As a matter of fact, the more intense these fusions are, the less tendency they have to expand, and the more widespread they are, the less tendency they have to intensify. This is why Communions are usually actualized in very narrow circles, while Masses are capable of being extended to the very largest numbers. Also, it is when the partial fusion is maintained at the middle degree of strength and depth (as in Community) that it appears easiest to establish a balance between unity and extension, that is to say, between intensity and volume. In other words, a we-ness which is constricted and intensified into Communion risks losing size and extension; inversely, if it is slackened and eased into the Mass, it is possible to expand and enlarge it without limits.

(c) *Finally, the intensity of the fusion in the We-ness and the force of attraction which it exercises over its members corresponds exactly. It is here and here only that the correlation is positive.* In fact, the force of attraction exercised by the we-ness is felt more because this we-ness penetrates farther into the depths of the self and the others, thus realizing a more intense participation. It is thus, aside from all other considerations, that Communion exercises a much stronger force of attraction over its members than does Community, and Community in its turn attracts its participants with more force than does Mass.

These considerations permit the unveiling of the origin of dogmatic prejudices which seek to establish an *a priori* evaluative hierarchy between Mass, Community and Communion. If one reasoned in this way, one would immediately confuse the point of view on participants, the point of view of "those who remain outside" and that of the sociological observer. The sociologist would give evidence of a naive over-simplification if, in order to infer the value of different we-nesses, he permitted himself to be guided by what the concerned members see in these. Let us take, first of all, the example of Communion. As soon as one passes from the effective participants to the hesitant, recalcitrant, to the indifferent, excluded or adversaries, the charm is broken. The Communion seems to them to exercise, not the minimum, but the maximum pressure; it appears as a center not of attraction, but of menacing oppression; as a source not of freedom, but of servitude. The dual internal and external aspect of Communion thus reveals its ambiguous, ambivalent character. Dogma and contrary speculative valuations have been made possible by this dual character which at the very outside sociologists ought to make a point of repudiating. Specifically, to tie Communion to the universal, as Bergson has done once again, is to detach it completely from social reality. As a matter of fact, it is precisely communion that has the strongest tendency to separation and to limitation and by this very fact, constitutes centers much less propitious to "universality" (always relative) than Mass and even Community. This is confirmed in the phenomenon of schism and secession which always threatens Communion as an actual manifestation of sociability. Nor should Communion be considered to have more truth and value in its contents. One can become a communicant in false ideas and negative values (Communion among criminals) the same as Mass can serve as centers of true ideas and positive values (the Mass we-ness of partisans for peace, for example). The fact that the medium degree of we-ness, community, tends toward more balance between volume (extension) pressure and attraction over its members, does not constitute an evaluative criterion. The tendency toward balance can do harm and become a source of immobility as well as of change. It is not for the sociologist to decide if a more or less strong pressure, a more or less freeing attraction or more or less balance between the two, even if it were effective, would be preferable in itself for social reality. This would depend essentially on circumstances, situations, structures of groups and societies, the types of the latter and on conjunctures.

Sociology, as well as philosophy, should resist all temptation to fix a hierarchy that is universally valid between Mass, Community and Communion; it is impossible to establish such an hierarchy. It is necessary to eliminate all evaluative implications in these degrees of We-ness. It is especially necessary to free the term "Mass" from all disparaging meaning and the term "Communion" from all eulogistic signification.

The distinction between Mass, Community and Communion can be confirmed in pointing out that, placing all other considerations aside, that among their levels, Mass has a tendency to accentuate attitudes, while Community tends to accentuate patterns and rules, and Communion, mental states and acts. Likewise, one notes that Community is more favorable to law and organized expressions than the two other degrees of We-ness. In the domain of moral life, Mass tends to favor the morality of ideal symbolic images or the morality of aspiration while Community favors imperative morality or the morality of virtue and Communion favors traditional morality or the morality of creation. In the cognitive sphere, Mass inclines preferentially towards representation, Community towards conceptualization, communion towards intuition.

TIME BELONGING TO MASS SOCIABILITY

Mass sociability has a tendency to move in erratic time, a diffuse time of irregular pulsations, of unforeseeable fluctuations between the appearance and disappearance of rhythms. This is particularly true here because among the depth levels, that of attitudes is especially favored. We already know that attitudes have a tendency to move in erratic time. This time of Mass sociability is often combined with deceptive time, which, while appearing to be of long duration, slowed down and sometimes calm, hides an explosive seething. Passive Masses move principally in the first of these times, the active Masses in the second.

In the time where passive Masses unfold, continuity appears to have a choice place, but it is interrupted by unexpected pulsation; furthermore the present, if not the past, seems to resist the future. Also, duration prevails over succession and often manifests itself in the collective memory and even more in the historical memory. In the time which the active Masses produce and where they move discontinuity is predominant. It is tried not only to the intensity of pulsations, but also to the time of aspiration, in advance of itself, and even to the explosive time of creation. The future then tends to become present, or more precisely to be projected into the present. Succession takes precedence over duration. The time of 'myths' (in the Sorelian meaning of the term)[1] and Utopia asserts itself in place of the time of collective and historic memory.

Whether Mass is passive or active, its time is first real and then experienced. But does this mean that mass sociability involves a clear *consciousness of time*? Is it a matter here of time perceived, time represented, time symbolized, time conceptualized? If so, at what point does Mass sociability succeed in mastering its time?

Let us say bluntly, the passive masses are not capable of becoming conscious of time in the proper meaning of the term, nor do they make the least attempt to master their time. They produce a specific time and move in this time, but they do not take account of the time in which they live. They are carried by the flow of time, but do not try to master it.

It is different with active masses. In their impatience and their initiative, they become conscious of the time they produce and in which their movement is unfolded. They not only experience time, they perceive it, and can even represent it, without going as far as symbolizing it. In the best cases, they accept the already completed symbolizations of the social classes or global societies where they are actualized. As far as mastering time, they may try to do it but certainly not by establishing a hierarchy of time. They master their time in certain unusual moments in the existence of classes and global societies, forcing the hand of the future in order to impose it over the present and the past. However, they do not always succeed here. It also happens that they attempt, but with still less success, to force the past on the present.

COMMUNITY SOCIABILITY AND ITS TIME

The time produced by *Community* is very different from that of Mass sociability. It is sometimes in advance, sometimes retarded, but delay dominates over advance, and here time alternating between delay and advance plays its part. A heated competition often takes place in the actualization of past and future in the present. This is confirmed, among other things, by the fact, that Community tends to favor the depth level of signs, signals, patterns, rules, and sometimes also of symbols and even of

---

[1] See note on page 99 for an explanation of this concept.

organization. Also Community often leans on a more stable ecological base than does mass sociability. Since the depth level of rules and patterns tends to move in a time alternating between delay and advance, this time finds added support in Community. Furthermore, because of symbols and organization, time held back on itself is more likely to be affirmed than time moving ahead.

Moreover, in Community time, continuity and discontinuity, past, present and future are all inclined to attain equivalence and balance. It is obvious in passive Community, and even more obvious in Community submerged in the unconscious, that continuity and time of slowed down, long duration are the most accentuated. In active Community alternating time, time moving forward, and retarded time are emphasized. But granting that Community tends towards a balance between activity and passivity, it moves in a mixed and ambivalent time. Often there is a very precarious equilibrium between present, past and future. As a rule, the time of Community more than the time of Mass and Communion, depends on the time of groups and global societies in which it is integrated. Likewise, it depends more than Mass and Communion on the time of special activities (economic, political, religious, juridical, etc...) which center in Communities.

Let us take as examples, on the one hand, the passive community of people speaking the same language and, on the other hand, the active community which is actualized in a Nation, in a local group, in a factory. Passive Communities neither directly perceive nor represent the time in which they live. But penetrated as they are by patterns, symbols, signals, etc., which are not their own for the most part, they become indirectly aware of the accentuated continuity of time which they produce and in which they live. In contrast, because they are manifested as centers of diverse and balanced conscious mental states and acts and because they favor the organized expressions of sociability, and even a certain rational and reflective character of the mentality, the active communities possess a reinforced capacity to become aware of their social time. Their tendency to persist in the face of change, and sometimes owing to change, prompts them to this. Not only the representation and the symbolization of real and experienced time, but also the effort to conceptualize and even to measure time, is first manifested in the atmosphere of Community. And how could it be otherwise, since Community generally favors judgments, conceptualizations, the cognitive, intellectual life? Obviously, these tendencies can only be observed indirectly, through the medium of groups and global societies where Community predominates. Examples are the ancient cities, the towns of the middle ages, locality or economic groupings. It is also active Community which manifests a continuing tendency to *master its time*. It does this by trying to balance the alternations between retarded time and time in advance. All other factors aside, it tends to approach this balance by orienting itself in the direction of a prudent slowing down and moderation of its time. In trying to master time, Community favors the present and ordinarily joins it together with the past, turning it away as much as possible from the future. In short, the effort of Community to master its time is characterized by a slightly conservative tendency; it does not intend to stop time, but rather to exclude from it the unforeseeable and render it as continuous as possible in order to make duration prevail over succession.

TIME CHARACTERISTIC OF COMMUNION SOCIABILITY

The time which *Communion* produces and in which it evolves differs from the time of Masses as well as from that of Communities. As the time of Masses is diffuse and is somewhat resistant to the awareness of it, and as the time of communities is balanced and appears to allow a possibility of being conceptualized as well as mastered, so the time of Communions is concentrated and reveals a propelling tendency. As a rule, communions are inclined to move in a time ahead of itself, sometimes going as far as explosive time, sometimes merely manifesting itself as a rushing and tense time. But this time, having a dense, concentrated character, turns in on itself. These "ecstasies of the future" easily turn into cyclical time, a kind of "frozen" dance on one spot, to which advance offers no outlet. Future, present and past are then mutually projected in one another, which leads the continuity of duration to dominate over the discontinuity of succession. This is the danger which threatens all Communions, when they do not successfully renew, surpass and transcend themselves. Their time, appearing to be in advance in itself, gives a false impression which conceals a camouflaged time of delay, as the future rejoins the past.

Such is the time of the passive communion of men who are faithful to the words of their Master, notably the mystic Communions, Communions of the devout who practice and observe a tradition. In these cases, all advance of time is only simulated in the end, and these Communions produce and move in a cyclical time of dance around the bush. However, even the active, and sometimes rational Communions of revolutionary minorities, Communions of researchers or of philosophers are overwhelmed by the time which they generate or in which they live.

The more active and inventive the Communions are, the less they endure. Their time in advance of itself, and sometimes even explosive time, do not permit them any rest, or, to pun, *their time does not give them any time*. Thus their decisive and successive instants are threatened with disintegration in cyclical time, if not in erratic time. This is why the time of active Communion does not endure and is constantly threatened with a crumbling away, in the very same way that the Communions themselves are threatened in their existence.

As Masses favor the depth level of attitudes, which are often unconscious, and Communities favor the rules, patterns, and symbols, so the Communions emphasize the level of collective ideas and values, whether or not these are combined with symbols. We have noted that the time of this level is a time of intense struggle between advance and delay in which neither alternation nor compromise is achieved. This is also the case with the time of communion which oscillates between a time in advance of itself susceptible to contact with the explosive time of creation, and cyclical time masking the greatest delay. The time of Communion, then, is never in equilibrium.

Do Communions become aware of the time which they produce and in which they live? Do they try to master their own time? As far as becoming aware of their time is concerned, only the passive, mystic communions have some chance of grasping it, perceiving it, and even of symbolizing it. However, this symbolization scarcely surpasses the cyclical time which makes them dance on one spot.

Active Communions, particularly the Communions of rational action, rarely succeed in grasping their own time, that is the time in which they live. They do not "have time" to *perceive* it, *represent* it, *symbolize* it. They can only revolt against all representations, symbolizations, conceptualizations and measures of time in the society in which they live.

As for the mastery of time, the passive Communions, and particularly the mystic Communions, can achieve it by trying to dissolve a large part of their time in ceremonies, periods of feasts and celebrations, and fêtes. These dominate the Communion rather than are mastered by Communion.

Active Communions also do not have the capacity to dominate their own time which escapes them. What they try to do (and sometimes they succeed) is to overturn the time and the scales of times of groups, classes, and global societies in which they are released. But they are *possessed by the time which they produce and where they move rather than mastering it.* Communions do not successfully master time, except for certain very exceptional moments such as a successfully accomplished revolution or an unusual collective discovery.

THE TIME CHARACTERISTIC OF APPROACH, WITHDRAWAL
AND MIXED INTERPERSONAL AND INTERGROUP RELATIONS

Our frame of reference now is sociability by partial opposition, that is intergroup as well as interpersonal relations with Others.

Relations of withdrawal tend to produce an erratic time, a time of irregular intervals between the appearance and disappearance of rhythms and a time alternating between advance and delay. Withdrawal ranges from separation of partners, recoil, temporary isolation, to conflicts, struggles, rejections, antagonisms, hostilities, and systematic hatreds, passing through jealousies, temporary or enduring quarrels, competition and rivalry. There are interpersonal relations or relations between We-nesses, groups, classes and global societies. This movement flows in an agitated time, full of discontinuity, where present and the future, sometimes projected in the past are out of balance. Relations of withdrawal, which most often are active relations, tend to move in a brusque and uncertain time. Prejudices, phobias, whims, racial and national myths, which so often poison the co-existence of groups and classes, intervene in passive withdrawal. Here, in addition to the time mentioned above, we find time held back and time of long duration and slow motion. There is no awareness of time in withdrawal relations.

Opposite to these are the relations of approach, beginning with attractions, affinities, like interests, passing through gifts, mutual or unilateral concessions and arriving at friendships and agreements between individuals, and between the we-nesses, groups, or global societies. These rela-

63

tions of approach move slowly and do not tolerate abruptness. Thus the time generated by approach and in which it moves is a time of delay combined with a time of long duration and slow motion. In relations of approach, there is only a relative intervention of the opposition between passive and active sociability with no particular repercussion on time. Here also awareness of time does not appear.

Intermediary are the *mixed relations* between individuals, we-nesses, groups and global societies. We define *mixed relations* as those found midway between approach and withdrawal, when simultaneously one approaches while withdrawing, and withdraws while approaching. This occurs in barter, contracts, property returns, credit, mortgages and different kinds of promises.

Mixed relations between the we-nesses, groups, classes and societies are for the most part *active relationships* in contrast to those which are established between individuals. They favor all kinds of patterns, signs, practices, symbols, communication, discussion, bargaining, all kinds of negotiations. Time produced by these mixed relations is also a mixed and combined time, time moving forward for the conclusion of the contract, which is often too hasty, time held back for fulfilment..., especially deceptive time with respect to the foundation of the relation. As a matter of fact, the terms of a mortgage, the clauses of a contract, etc., tend to be overthrown by the factual conditions in which the parties are involved at the moment of the execution of the contract. Furthermore, the clauses or terms of the contract are made to endure as long as possible, to commit the future and thus impede change, unless a new agreement occurs between the partners. The new agreement is not always easy to obtain. In the time of contractual relation intervening between deceptive, delayed and advancing time, continuity is strongly accentuated favoring past and present while projecting them toward the future.

The active, mixed relations between the we-nesses, groups, classes, societies, are the only relations with Others in which time intervening here admits the possibility of becoming aware of time and mastering it. Not only do these relations generate a particular social time, but they are driven to know it, perceive it, represent it, symbolize it. It is true that here they depend largely on collectivities, groups, and global societies where they are integrated. But they contribute in their turn to the awareness of time by collectivities, groups and global societies. In the mastery of time, the mixed relations make a striking effort to subject the future to the present and even to the past.

Obviously, the situation is very different when it is a matter of passive mixed relations, which are ambiguous and ambivalent and whose time remains undecipherable. Here the interpersonal relations predominate over the relations between collectivities.

CHAPTER V

THE PARTICULAR GROUPINGS AND
THEIR SOCIAL TIME

We move on from the micro-social scale to the first manifestation of macro-social collective units, the particular groupings. It is important to distinguish these clearly from the social classes and global societies, which are both macrocosms of groupings.

We define the groups as real, but partial, collective units. They can be observed directly, are based on collective attitudes and continuous and active conduct, and have collective works to accomplish. The unity of collective attitudes, works and conducts constitutes a structurable social framework in which the manifestations of sociability tend towards relative cohesion.

In the social framework of the group the centripetal forces predominate, to a certain degree at least, over the centrifugal forces, and unity prevails over plurality. There is a strong tendency for a certain cohesion to sweep over the divergent we-nesses and over the different relations with Others. Thus, the unity of the group cannot be reduced to its depth levels nor to the plurality of manifestations of sociability which move in the interior of groups.

All groupings are structurable, but they are not all structured. Thus, the economic strata, the unemployed, the age groupings of generations, publics, crowds, etc., finally collectivities of producers and consumers can constitute groups. They are not reduced to simple categories, aggregates or collections of individuals although these groupings are only very rarely structured.

However, most groups, whether they are organized or unorganized, are expressed in a *structure*, that is, "in an uncertain equilibrium between multiple hierarchies of depth levels, manifestations of sociability, social regulations, and mental colorations. This balance is rendered conscious and sustained by the cultural works cementing it". Where organizations exist, they only participate in the equilibrium of structure, but never succeed in expressing it sufficiently. Thus the structure of a family, of a professional group, of a state, of a Church, is not to be identified with

66

their organizations, nor with their total social phenomena. Much closer to the latter than to the former, it is in fact neither one nor the other of these two layers of social reality.

We shall return later to the structure problem when we shall treat the variations of time belonging to classes and to global societies. These are structured, and yet never express themselves in a single organization. All that should be emphasized here is that, in spite of appearances to the contrary, the time in which groups, even structured groups move, is not more continuous nor more easily quantified than time in other social frameworks. This is so even though the groupings tend to be characterized by continuity of attitudes, works and conduct and even though the structured groupings are distinguished by a balance of multiple hierarchies. Two facts explain this: (1) constant effort is required to unify a particular grouping, (2) all structure resembles only the outer shell of a carcass – inside there is a movement of structuration, destructuration, restructuration, as well as explosive breakdown at some turns. Furthermore, the time of the depth levels and of the manifestations of sociability within the groupings and still more yet the time of classes and of global societies surrounding them, penetrate groupings, in different degrees, with their dash, their ecstasies, with their rhythms. Thus none of the kinds of social time can be excluded from particular groupings, whether structured or not. It is necessary to confront the groupings with all the kinds of time.

THE CRITERIA FOR CLASSIFICATION OF GROUPS

We have proposed a general classification of particular groupings according to many different criteria.[1] Some of these criteria, such as that of the *duration* (temporary, durable and permanent groupings) and the *rhythm* (groupings of slow, medium, or precipitated cadence) are directly related to time. The others, which treat the extent of a group's dispersion, the manner of admission, the functions, the orientation, the degrees of unity, serve well as frameworks for producing the social time in which their existence flows.

This general classification of groupings is essentially pragmatic, and is only useful to the degree it can offer a frame of reference for empirical

[1] Cf. *La vocation actuelle de la sociologie*, Vol. I, 3rd ed., 1963, pp. 308–357.

inquiries and research, as suggestions for experiments and socio-historical reconstructions, both leading to explanation. The fifteen criteria proposed to distinguish these groupings, overlap for the most part and the number can be augmented or diminished according to the domain and field of research or to the situation in the social reality itself. Equal importance should not be attributed to all the proposed group distinctions, but should depend on the concern of the study: sociology of law, sociology of moral life, sociology of knowledge, etc., or research into the manifestations of sociability favored by the groups, their sociological determinisms, or the multiplicity of their social time (as we are doing in this book) the study of social classes or the global societies. This is so true that only a selection is required in this book dedicated to the sociology of time. However, before noting the group distinctions necessary for study, we shall remind the reader of the complete scheme of our classification:

1. Content:
    (a) Uni-functional groupings
    (b) Multi-functional groupings
    (c) Supra-functional groupings

2. Size:
    (a) Small
    (b) Medium
    (c) Extended

3. Duration:
    (a) Temporary
    (b) Enduring
    (c) Permanent

4. Rhythm:
    (a) Slow cadence
    (b) Medium cadence
    (c) Rapid cadence

5. Degree of dispersion:
    (a) Groupings at a distance (non-assembled groupings)

(b) Groupings of artificial media contact (letters, newspapers, journals, etc.)

(c) Groupings assembled periodically

(d) Groupings in permanent meeting

6. Basis of formation:
   (a) *De fait*
   (b) Voluntary
   (c) Enforced

7. Ease of admission:
   (a) Open
   (b) Conditional admission
   (c) Closed

8. Degree of externalization:
   (a) Unorganized, non-structured groupings
   (b) Unorganized, structured groupings
   (c) Partially organized groupings
   (d) Completely organized groupings
   (c and d above involve organization as an element of their structure)

9. Function:
   (a) Kinship
   (b) Fraternal
   (c) Locality
   (d) Economic activity
   (e) Groupings midway, between fraternal and economic activity, for instance, the "strata"
   (f) Non-remunerative activities
   (g) Mystic-ecstatic

10. Orientation:
    (a) Devisive
    (b) Unifying

11. Degree of penetration by the global society:

(a) Groupings resisting penetration by the global society
(b) Groupings more or less submissive to penetration by the global society
(c) Groupings completely submissive to penetration by the global society

12. Degree of compatibility between groupings:
    (a) Complete compatibility between groupings of the same type
    (b) Partial compatibility between groupings of the same type
    (c) Incompatibility between groupings of the same type
    (d) Exclusive groupings

13. Mode of constraint:
    (a) Groupings commanding conditional constraint
    (b) Groupings commanding unconditional constraint

14. Principles governing organization:
    (a) Groupings of domination
    (b) Groupings of collaboration

15. Degree of Unity:
    (a) Unitary groupings
    (b) Federal groupings
    (c) Confederate groupings

To study the problem of social time, we shall limit our discussion to groupings distinguished according to the criteria of duration, rhythm, degree of dispersion, admission, function, orientation and degree of unity. These seem to us to constitute the most fruitful frames of reference for our subject.

TIME OF GROUPINGS CLASSIFIED ACCORDING TO THEIR DURATION

Let us begin by examining the temporary, enduring and permanent groups from the point of view of the social time which they produce.

The term *temporary* designates groupings which are dissolved as soon as the particular task for which they were originally formed is considered accomplished. We can list as examples: (a) a crowd; (b) a conspiring or plottng group; (c) bands, such as the famous "*bandeirates*" in Brazil, temporary teams of explorers of countries, or groups searching for gold or uranium; (d) the partisans and the "*maquisards*" during World War II; (e) athletic teams formed for a single competition; teams of scientific researchers dedicated to special inquiries; (f) assemblies and meetings; (g) demonstrations. It is necessary in these latter two cases to distinguish meetings or demonstrations which are externalizations of durable groupings and those which are not; (h) play groups.

In which times do the temporary groupings tend to live? To answer this question three considerations are kept in mind. The temporary groups foresee their existence as limited and therefore they are in a hurry. They are thus inclined to live in a time in advance of itself. But their agitation is not always successful in finding the path between the present and future. More often the present is projected in the future than the future in the present. In this fashion, time in advance of itself is tied to erratic time. The depth levels of attitudes, innovating and effervescent conduct, ideas and values, mental states and acts are favored rather than the patterns, regulations, regulated conduct, organization and even symbols. This reinforces the relation of time in advance of itself with erratic time which also comes into contact with time alternating between advance and delay. The fact that Mass We-ness and Communion We-ness predominate in the heart of temporary groupings to the disadvantage of Community We-ness only intensifies the agitated character and violent fluctuations of the time of temporary groupings. Temporary groupings always live in an extremely tense and buffeted time where, in spite of all efforts, the predominant present is detached from the past and only loosely tied to the future.

Seeing that their existence is limited in time the temporary groupings are always aware of time. They grasp and perceive the time which they produce but they "do not have the time" to symbolize nor to conceptualize it. And although they are led to measure their time, they borrow the standards of this measurement from the global societies in which they are integrated. All the evidence indicates that the temporary groupings do not have the capacity to master their time. If they could do it, they would prolong their own existence and transform themselves into enduring groupings.

Enduring Groupings are dissolved only under certain conditions such as death, maturity, will, or by the agreement of the interested parties, the decision of the majority of the members, or by a dissolution imposed from the outside. The majority of groupings, from the household family, age-groups, to labor unions and political parties, businesses enterprise, trusts and cartels, are enduring groupings, but their duration varies according to their character and the circumstances.

The enduring groupings produce many very different times. It would not be fruitful to search for the particular time they tend to favor. But they do not generally favor erratic time nor explosive time. They are not always aware of the time they produce, and their effort to master time coincides with the mere effort to persist.

A *permanent grouping* is one whose dissolution is neither foreseen nor envisaged. This is the case with castes, professions, Churches, States, International Organizations, etc. These permanent groupings depend less than the others on the life and the will of their participants, whether these are individuals, the we-ness, or included groups. At the very core of their life, permanent groupings customarily emphasize the levels of organization, patterns and regulations. As a rule, community sociability rather than communion or mass sociability has more opportunity. This is why the permanent groupings favor time held back on itself and alternating time, combined with deceptive time, cyclical time, and time of long duration and slow motion. From this point of view there is a considerable difference between a permanent grouping such as the State and a permanent grouping such as the Church. The State, existing in alternating time, can bind itself to time in advance and even to explosive time, while the Church clearly leans toward the cyclical time turned in on itself.

The permanent groupings are led to awareness of the time which they produce and in which they live. They not only grasp and perceive these times, but they also try to symbolize, conceptualize, measure, and sometimes even quantify them. Are not calendars linked with these two permanent groupings, the Churches and the States? Both try to impose their time, their scales of time, their cadence, their rhythms of time on all the other groupings, and more broadly, on all the other social frameworks. This predisposes the States and the Churches to detach their time manifestations from their own frameworks and to consider them as universal and standardized. They also try to master their time and partially succeed in upholding their own scales of time against all the other groupings, including the global society as such. But this apparent success is only a veritable Pyrrhic victory. While mastering their own time, they do not succeed in mastering the time and the scales of time which surround them, which compete with them, and which threaten to make them explode. The time of the social classes and global societies, and the time of the different we-nesses and groups within them are often in conflict with the time of the State and of the Church.

The particular groupings distinguished according to their rhythms are the *groupings of slow, medium and rapid cadence.* Rhythm is a measure of time which does not destroy the specific character of its qualitative element, the convergency or divergency of its movements. *Rhythm is an accentuation of duration and intervals, seeking an equilibrium between continuity and discontinuity.* Halbwachs, who had the insight to insist on the divergent time of different groupings, unhappily failed to pay the least attention to the difference between their time and their rhythm.

Halbwachs' thesis concerning the social time of different groupings opened up new perspectives. He wrote: "There is not one universal and unique time. A society breaks down into a multiplicity of groups, each with its own duration." (*La mémoire collective*, 1950, pp. 126) and again: "Thus, there are as many origins of different times as there are groups. No one time is imposed on all groups." (Ibid., pp. 108). He entitled a whole section in his *La mémoire collective*, 'Multiplicity and Heterogeneity of Collective Durations' (pp. 103–110) and spoke of "their impermeability" (pp. 110–114). Finally, he insisted on the liaison of memory with the specific times of the groups (pp. 116–129).

However, after having spoken of the "multiplicity and the heterogeneity of collective durations," that is to say, of specific social times belonging to groups, Halbwachs appears to have identified them with simple rhythms. Thus in noting the divergency between the time which flows in the home, at school, in the office, factory or at church, in the trade-union, political party or village, the city, etc. Halbwachs seems finally to reduce the multiplicity of time to the difference in their rhythms and even to their calendars. There should be more to it than the calendars of different groupings. "It matters little that here and there one speaks of days, of months, of years. One group cannot use the calendar of another. The religious camp does not live in the market place and cannot find reference points there. If it were otherwise in the distant past, it was because economic groups were not yet detached from religious groups" (p. 110). However, to the degree that differences of time are reduced to differences of rhythms, and the latter to differences of calendars, a certain correspondence of these "durations" are established, even if only approximately. This helps the individual to move from one to another of these group times (pp. 104–110). This permits also a comparison of the slowness and speed of the times of different groups, although precautions ought to be taken in this comparison (Ibid, pp. 114–116).

Halbwachs's analyses of the rhythms of social time appear to be rigorously exact, but there are serious reservations to make when it is a matter of social time itself, where rhythms are often unfathomable. We can speak, even more firmly than did Halbwachs, of groupings with *slow, medium and rapid* "rhythm" or cadence of time, without identifying precisely the specific character of time that these groupings produce and in which they live.

Certain groupings have a more rapid time rhythm than others as some groups have continually changing characteristics and others scarcely vary at all. It is also the same for changes of goods, tools, patterns, and symbols which the groups utilize. American sociologists have applied the term *social mobility* to the more or less slow or accelerated circulation of the totality of these phenomena, usually to economic strata and to global society, but it is perfectly usable in the study of rhythms of movement of each group, if there is a rhythm.

At first glance, it appears that locality groupings like kinship groupings tend to move with a much slower rhythm than groupings of economic activity or fraternal groupings such as groupings of adolescents. It appears that the time rhythm of political parties and of trade-unions is more rapid than that of States, which in turn is more rapid than that of Churches. The organized Churches appear to move with a slower rhythm than the sects and even religious orders.

However, all these generalizations only serve as indicators to guide the description of specific movements of groupings, situated in a global structure and in a concrete conjuncture. An analysis still has to be made of these times (real, rendered conscious, mastered) whose slow, medium and rapid cadence are only imperfect expressions and measures.

Examples of groupings of rapid rhythms, are the economic strata within the social classes at the present time, factories and businesses with seasonal changes of personnel, and contemporary large cities. Which times do these groupings of rapid rhythms favor? They favor time alternating between advance and delay. And it is precisely this *alternation* which is *precipitated*, not the advance or the projection of the future in the present.

Examples of groupings of slow rhythm are villages isolated from large cities, permanent groupings such as the State and the Church, licensed professional groups such as those of physicians, lawyers, college and university faculties. They live in a time held back on itself, sometimes bound with time of long duration (the village), sometimes with cyclical time turned in on itself (the Church), sometimes with deceptive time (the State). Here the slow rhythm is restrained in order to accentuate the dominant traits of time of which rhythm is only a repercussion.

It need not be stressed that the groupings of medium rhythm, intermediate between precipitation and slowing down, (such as factories, unions, schools and universities, small cities, contemporary professions, yesterday's guilds, and so on), leave the door wide open to different social times and their varied scales.

In short, and paradoxically enough, the social frameworks made up of the groupings classified according to their social mobility or their slow, medium, or precipitated rhythm, yield a much poorer harvest than expected, as far as the study of their time, properly speaking, is concerned.

TIME OF GROUPS CLASSIFIED ACCORDING TO THEIR DISPERSION

The groupings distinguished according to the measure of their dispersion (non-assembled groupings, groupings of media contact, groupings meeting regularly, groups in continuous assemblage) serve as different frameworks of social time and merit attention.

The non-assembled groupings are made up not only of non-structured collective units, such as the unemployed, the producers, the different publics, but also of the professions and of social classes. Permanent groupings such as the Church and the State are intermediate between groupings meeting regularly and non-assembled groupings. All these groupings move in a time, sometimes held back, sometimes in pushing forward. The conflict between these two social times is intensified by the fact that non-assembled groupings, on the one hand, accent the level of symbols which reinforces the tendency toward the time held back, and, on the other hand, accent the level of collective mental acts, ideas and values, which propel them toward time in advance of itself. Likewise, all other considerations aside, the non-assembled groupings often are collectivities who favor the actualization of mass sociability. Nevertheless, this tendency can be reversed, and in certain historical events, communion sociability is favored in the non-assembled groupings. Now, if the mass sociability reinforces erratic time, communion sociability sometimes accentuates time in advance of itself, and sometimes cyclical time.

It is not surprising, then, that the social time of non-assembled groupings may be contradictory and multiple, and that the struggle between time in advance of itself and time held back can be added to deceptive time, erratic time and cyclical time.

Examples of groupings of media-contact are political parties, so far as their members do not attend periodical meetings, or committees which do not hold sessions, etc. They share the characteristics of the non-assembled groupings, except that special emphasis is given to the level of signs and symbols, which favors time held back on itself.

The non-assembled groupings and media-contact groupings neither favor nor shun awareness of time and the mastering of it. As a matter of fact, certain non-assembled groupings such as the permanent groupings and the social classes, are centers of awareness and mastery of time. Certain others, such as the groupings of unemployed, producers and consumers, different publics, are not such centers.

Groups meeting periodically can meet at fairly long intervals or very frequently, and even remain in a meeting a very large part of the day. Electoral bodies of the State, unions, political parties, cooperatives, societies of vested interests, etc., are of the first type; factories, offices, primary and high school classes, theatrical companies, etc., are of the second type. Groupings meeting periodically appear to favor alternating time. Groups which meet only rarely combine this time, either with cyclical time, or with deceptive time; while those which meet often move in alternating time which compromises with deceptive and erratic time.

These tendencies are reinforced by the fact that the groupings which meet periodically accentuate the level of rules, patterns, regular roles, as well as that of organization. Also community sociability tends to be actualized at their core. Now rules and patterns propel toward alternating time, and organizations propel toward deceptive time. In a like manner, Community favors alternating time while preferring delay over advance.

Groupings meeting periodically become aware of their time, grasp it and perceive it, but do rarely attempt to symbolize ,it or to conceptualize it. For this, they generally have confidence in the global society in which they are integrated or in the permanent groups on which they depend. However, they are faced with the problem of the mastery of their time. It consists in the effort either to maintain the regularity of meetings, or to modify it, or sometimes to transform themselves into permanently convened groups or into non-assembled groups.

Intimate groupings permanently convened include such groupings as domestic families, households, small hamlets, boarding schools, convents, etc. In spite of their apparent regular and rather slow cadence, these groupings often live in a time of irregular pulsations and intense fluctuation. Their resistance to organization which can be imposed on them and their tendency to actualize Communion in certain moments of their existence, only reinforces their push towards the time of irregular pulsations, sometimes combined with deceptive time and cyclical time, limited by slowed down time.

TIME OF GROUPS CLASSIFIED ACCORDING TO MODE OF ADMISSION

Groupings distinguished according to their admission policy are open, conditional admission and closed groupings. We can now consider them as frameworks for specific social time.

Open groupings have no precise requirements for admission. These are the various groupings *de fait* and also certain voluntary groupings such as rescue teams, certain philanthropic groups, public meetings, as well as certain groups established by the State such as communes, municipalities, primary schools, which have no barriers.

Closed and exclusive groupings, almost impossible to enter, were prevalent in types of societies other than ours. The gens, phratries, eupatrides and the patricians, the curia, clans, and matrimonial groups in various archaic societies; castes in India are examples of closed groupings of imposed character. Among the voluntary closed groupings are the trade guilds during the second half of the Middle Ages, certain clubs, secret societies, conspiracies and plots resolved not to admit anyone else. These cases are rather exceptional in contemporary society. We can however mention certain trusts and cartels, the famous "200 families", in France before World War II, the groups of nobility or the *haute bourgeoisie* which only recruit by birth or heritage.

Most other groupings are groupings of conditional access. Obviously the conditions of admission are extremely varied from the very difficult to the very easily realizable. They can require magic tests involving a risk of life property qualifications, different procedures of cooptation or election, as those which are required for becoming members of faculties and learned societies and for being admitted to the bar, etc. In the latter cases, beyond cooptation, specific diplomas are required, tests or a presentation of a dissertation, which in itself constitutes a condition of admission: thus sometimes serious limits arise for entry into a profession or into an establishment.

Open groupings, which sometimes lack internal coherence, do not reverberate directly on the time, nor normally produce a specific time or scale of time. They leave the doors wide open to all and sundry social times, to groupings distinguished according to other criteria, to social classes or finally, to global society.

The closed groupings, on the contrary, tend to produce time of long duration and slow motion, sometimes cyclical time, and finally, time held back on itself. This is why one often says that closed groups do not live "in their time", or that they live "beyond their time". In certain cases they can also be characterized as attempts to place themselves "outside time".

The inclination of closed groupings toward a time of long duration turned in on itself, is reinforced by the accentuation of rigid and fixed traditions, of esoteric and hermetic symbols, and of an intolerant mentality. This accentuation of tradition is not meshed with the possible actualization of the Communion sociability in these groups, as passive and often semi-conscious communion is favored in which cyclical time is only a camouflage for delay.

As a framework for social time, the groupings of conditional access draw nearer to the closed groupings, or to the open groupings according

78

to the requirements for admission. When it is a matter of cooptation based on examinations and diplomas, an appreciation of professional and moral qualities, time alternating between delay and advance is emphasized. The selected constituencies, the groupings of this type (for example, the bar, the order of physicians, the faculties of an university) can, in certain circumstances, encourage the time in advance of itself (discoveries, new initiatives). But the formality of requirements, the rules of the game of recruitment, and the inevitable limitations of the strata and classes from which the selection takes place push toward the time held back. This tendency to favor the time alternating between delay and advance with delay somewhat preferred, is reinforced by the fact that the groupings of more or less severe cooptation at base, accentuate the level of patterns, rules, symbols, and actualize community sociability more often than mass and communion sociability. This sometimes leads deceptive time to mask the time in advance of itself so the latter can be more developed. Thus, for example, Institutes, Academies and Faculties, live in a time held back, so that scientific discoveries and innovations can be furthered only with precaution or frequently arise outside of the groups where admission is rather difficult.

Closed groupings and most of the groupings of conditional access become aware of the time in which they live and try to master it. The closed groupings grasp, perceive and sometimes represent, symbolize and conceptualize their time in their own way, often contrary to the time of the global societies in which they are integrated. This awareness of time tends to be tied to the collective memory and still more to historical memory. It evokes or glorifies mythological time or simply the "good old days" when the closed groupings were licensed and enjoyed special influence or at least possessed power or exercised domination. This happened with the upper castes, groups of priests, the eupatrides and patricians, nobility, and can be observed even today in the upper-strata of the bourgeois class.

Closed groupings are forced to master time in resisting all times other than their own, and in doing their utmost to arrest the course of time, to sublimate it in "living eternity", indestructable, defying the interference of time of other groups and even that of the global society.

Groupings with more or less difficult access, particularly the groupings of cooptation, also become aware of their own time and try to master it. Here, above all, the mastery of time consists in the specific periodicity of time: for example, time of the passage through secondary education; time of preparing the academic career; time of the stage in the higher educational system in the provinces; time of arrival and activity in the Paris University. It is not a matter of a simple specific calendar of periods of life of the members of higher education, but of the effort to maintain a balance in alternating between delay and advance, all the while taking into account scientific and pedagogical merits.

TIME OF GROUPS CLASSIFIED BY FUNCTIONS

We can now turn to the groupings distinguished according to their functions, that is according to the tasks which they have to accomplish, in order to see how these groups operate as frameworks of social time.

In previous publications we distinguished the following six groupings according to their functions:

(1) *Kinship groupings* based either on blood relatives or on mythological ancestors. Closer to us, the domestic extended families often represent case-limits between kinship groupings and groupings of economic activity; also there are the conjugal families, the household families of today, etc.

(2) *Fraternal groupings*, based as much on affinity of situation (including the economic situation, as for example, the economic strata in the interior of social classes) as on the affinity of belief, tastes, interests. Examples are groupings of age and sex, male puberty groupings in the archaic societies, the groupings of people earning the same salary or possessing similar incomes or fortunes, the different publics, fraternities, friendships, cooperatives, etc...,

(3) *Locality groupings*, of a territorial character, whose members are tied to the neighborhood and the necessity of maintaining arrangements in the place where they live, such as the cities (large and small), the villages and the hamlets, the communes, the municipalities, departments, regions, States, etc...

(4) *Groupings of economic activity*, that is all groupings whose principle function consists in participation in production, exchange, the distribution of wealth or in the arrangement of consumption. Such are the professions, farms, workshops, factories, shops, stores, trade societies, business and banking concerns, trusts, cartels, and so on. Also numerous cases exist intermediate between the groupings of economic activity and

kinship groupings, as well as groupings which combine the characteristics of fraternal groupings with those of economic activity. In addition to the economic strata and consumer and producer cooperatives, we can list the teams workers in a factory, labor unions and the non-hierarchized professions, etc...

(5) *Groupings of non-remunerative activities:* political parties, learned societies, artistic societies, pedagogical associations, civic associations, philanthropic societies and foundations, literary and scientific clubs, athletic associations.

(6) *Mystic-ecstasy groupings:* Churches, congregations, religious orders, convents, sects, magic brotherhoods, masonic lodges, etc...

Some of these groups overlap the groupings about which we have already spoken in conjunction with other distinctions. This is the case with Churches and States which we have already examined as frameworks of social time in our analysis of permanent groupings and non-assembled groupings. That is why we are going to choose examples from among the groupings about which we have not yet or not sufficiently spoken.

The kinship groupings have a tendency to move in a time of long duration and slow motion limited by erratic time, characteristic of intimate groupings permanently convened. The time of long duration and slow motion is reinforced by the fact that these groupings accentuate, on one hand, the depth levels of the unconscious and subconscious mental states of affective character where the collective memory is nourished, and on the other hand, the ecological base. The actualization in their midst of passive community sociability has the same effect. Obviously the situation changes when it is a matter of the domestic family tied to economic activity, and more broadly in the case of family enterprises. It is necessary to add that when both of the spouses of a household work outside the home, the family group often tends to be dissolved into the simple relations with Others, producing erratic time unless their time depends on the groupings where each spouse is individually integrated. The Kinship groupings are not usually aware of their time and do not make any effort to master it.

Fraternal groupings often tend to move in a time in advance of itself, which is sometimes illusory; in this case it becomes a time of imaginative facility due to their affinity; time which does not always find a passage towards the future and only projects the present towards it. However, the time of fraternal groupings tends to accentuate discontinuity: for example, the discontinuity of generations, of the present and the future, and so on. According to the circumstances, this time can be linked with erratic or cyclical time. This tendency towards the time jerked by the irregularity of intervals is indeed reinforced by accentuation of the depth levels of uncertain and hesitant opinions, of the confict between economic interests and the unforeseen social roles, accompanied, in the microsocial domain, by the actualization of community and of communion, now active, now passive. When adolescents constitute an effective group, these uncertainties of social time generated by the fraternal groupings emerge with particular intensity. Fraternal groupings can sometimes become aware of their time, in perceiving its advance and the opportunities to precipitate it; this is why these groups can become impatient, but they never acquire mastery of their time.

The locality groupings tend to produce a time held back, often reinforced by its liaison with time of long duration. Only the State, on the one hand, and the large cities, on the other hand, are exceptions here and have to be placed apart. The tendency of the locality groupings to favor the time held back is intensified by the accentuation in their midst of the depth level of rules and rigid patterns and of standardized symbols, on the one hand, and of the ecological-geographical level on the other hand, and by their actualization of the microsocial element of community. When the organized level is also brought out sharply – which is ordinarily the case in locality groupings – the time held back is somewhat reinforced. Added, however, is deceptive time or time of surprise, from which organizations never succeed in escaping.

The groupings of economic activity tend to produce a time where advance and delay, future and present are in conflict or in competition, often never even enter into a pitched battle, usually without arriving at an effective alternation. However, at certain turning points, which are much more frequent than the opposite situations, the time moving forward is victorious and can even enter into contact with the explosive time of creation. This is because the groupings of economic activity are always linked with labor and techniques. These two, carried along by their own dynamism,unchain in their turn the movement of the economic groupings. As soon as the economic groupings are differentiated from family and locality groupings and the more they become separated, time moving forward begins to threaten time held back. This time of the economic groupings enters into conflict with the time of the other groups. However, here erratic time often counteracts time moving forward and thus indirectly reinforces the delayed time in these groupings. Economic groupings depend on the one hand, on property relations and the organized super-structure, and on the other hand, on technical patterns, procedures and inventions. Thus they accentuate the level of innovating conduct as well as the levels of patterns, rules and organization. Alternating time and deceptive time is introduced here into the struggle between time moving forward and time held back. The time of groupings of economic activity is thus, finally, a particularly complex time, especially since they tend to actualize active community sociability – this can even lead towards a communion of effort, meeting an obstacle in the mass element which is sharply emphasized by all the assigned, imposed and enslaved common labor.

We can now summarize the question of the consciousness and mastery of time among the economic groupings. The groupings involved in economic activity have a tendency to be conscious of the time which they produce. They try to grasp it, to perceive, symbolize and conceptualize it and even measure it. They attempt also to gain mastery over their time. Their consciousness of time is realized in such terms as delivery date, productivity, value, salary-price, as well as joy in work, weariness, saturation, need for a "break", recreation and leisure. A major concern of economic groupings is the effort to manage time. This is manifested in the various attempts to have *the early* dominate *the late* or *vice-versa*. On the other hand, we see this effort to manage time involved in a struggle to relate it to the time standards of the global society. These are the standards which permit the establishment of a general scale of productivity involving value-salary, wage-price, circulation and exchange of goods.

The groupings which have no monetary gain function, only produce their own time when they are divisive groupings such as political parties, or academic societies representing a particular scientific or philosophical position. Otherwise, they are dominated by the times of other groups or the global society to which they belong.

Finally, the time favored by the mystic-ecstatic groupings is a cyclical-time which is turned in on itself, where future and past, early and late are reunited and all revolve in an endless circle. The actualization of mystic communions in these groupings has the same result. Ecstatic groupings accentuate the level of rites, modified by practices, and of basic affective symbols which are sustained by certain specific mental states and mental acts ("intuitional beliefs" and acts of "mystic participation"). This leads to the liaison of their cyclical time with time rather behind itself and with the time of long duration. This may or may not be reinforced by the organization level. Only under exceptional circumstances do mystic-ecstatic groupings combine with the time ahead of itself. These exceptional circumstances are found in new religious movements, manifestations of messianic hope, heresies and sharp conflicts between magic and religion.

In the mystic-ecstatic groups the consciousness of time and the effort to master it are linked with the timetable for celebrating the rites and festivals. The consciousness of time and its mastery go in two directions simultaneously and, thus, are dominated by a paradox: on the one hand, there is the desire to sacrifice real time to eternity, be it living eternity or a static eternity; on the other hand, there is the desire to maintain set phases for the cycles and festivals which leads to the measurement of time by calendars. Churches serve as important examples of this latter tendency.

TIME OF GROUPINGS CLASSIFIED ACCORDING TO
THEIR ORIENTATION

Divisive groupings have an orientation toward struggle; the unifying groupings (*groupings of union*) *have a conciliatory orientation.* Every grouping, with two exceptions, can go both ways. One exception is represented by the social classes, those supra-groupings or macrocosms of groupings, about which we shall speak specifically in the next chapter. They are always divisive groupings. The other exception is represented by the groupings of locality, culminating in the political States. They are always, in principle, unifying groupings. With the exception of these two all other groupings only manifest tendencies in one direction or the other. Their trend can be reversed under certain conditions. Normally, groupings of the fraternal type such as political parties, crafts, professional associations, labor unions and employer alliances, producers or consumers so far as they constitute real collective units, are divisive groupings. Likewise magical fraternities, sects and religious orders fit in this category. In contrast, factories, business enterprises, industries, organizations for general economic planning, social insurance bodies, along with universal churches are customarily unifying groupings.

It would be unwarranted to confuse this distinction with "groupings serving the general interest or a particular interest". For the general interest, being only an equilibrium between opposing interests, can be served by divisive groupings and hindered by unifying groupings including States and churches.

Divisive groupings are, generally speaking, more capable of intense life, show more initiative and innovations. They tend to accentuate the levels of mental acts (judgments and intuitions), values and ideas, and active communion more than do the unifying groupings. The latter are more traditional, more continuous, more apt to be structured, and regulated by norms and patterns. They are more apt to accentuate these latter depth levels as well as to actualize community sociability.

Consequently, the divisive groupings tend to produce time in advance where the future is rendered present. This time can be linked with erratic time and explosive time. In contrast, the unifying groupings lean towards retarded time where the *present* is projected into the future and which is often linked with the time of long duration and slow motion. Moreover cyclical time and deceptive time come into frequent conflict here, sometimes without any issue. The unifying groupings, therefore, normally live in a much more conservative time than the divisive groupings.

Consciousness of time is more acute in the divisive groupings than in the unifying groupings. The latter, nevertheless, on occasion, succeed in gauging their time better. The divisive groupings do not master their time but are rather carried away by it, which does not stop their frequent combat with the time of the global societies in which they live. In contrast, the unifying groupings make a great effort to master their time. The unification and conciliation towards which they are oriented depend, in general, on such mastery.

CHAPTER VI

THE SOCIAL CLASSES AND THEIR SCALES
OF SOCIAL TIME

In social classes as frameworks for social time we are confronted most vigorously with the problem of a scale of times or, in other words a hierarchy of multiple manifestations of time. A social class constitutes a universe, a collective whole which is so vast and rich that it can rival even the time of global society. From this point of view we face a paradox. While States and Churches strive to master their own time, as well as the time of all other groupings and even in some turns that of the global society (albeit never successfully), the social classes, although always conscious of their own specific time, usually do not have pretensions of mastering their time, or, above all, of imposing it on other classes. Nonetheless, they often succeed in doing this very thing. The social time scale of a rising class, particularly when it begins to take power, is imposed to a large degree on the whole of society. It is only afterwards that the global society reacts, by opposing its own time scale to that of the victorious social class. The complex dialectical game played between the time scale of a social class and the time scale of the global society which it is preparing to dominate or has already commenced to dominate, has been somewhat oversimplified by Marxian analysis. In this analysis there has been a tendency to reduce global society determinism to class determinism, and consequently the time scale of the global society has been reduced to the time scale of classes. More precisely, there has been a temptation to make these two time scales identical in Marxian analysis.

First we must define social class and distinguish it from particular groupings and from the global society. We begin with the definition offered in previous writings[1]:

Social classes are inclusive, particular supra-groupings of considerable breadth and scope, containing macrocosms of sub-groupings and partial macrocosms. The unity of classes, is dependent upon their supra-

---

[1] *Déterminismes sociaux et liberté humaine*, 2nd ed., 1963, pp. 193 ff.; see also *Le concept de classe sociale de Marx à nos jours*, 2nd ed., pp. 133 ff.; *La vocation actuelle de la sociologie* Vol. I, 3rd ed., 1963, pp. 357 ff., *Traité de sociologie*, Vol. I, 2nd ed., pp. 198 ff.

functionality, their resistance to penetration by the global society, their radical incompatibility with one another and their special cultural works. Their thrust towards structuration implies a predominant collective consciousness. These supra-groupings only appear in industrialized global societies where the technical patterns and economic activities are especially accentuated. They have the following traits: they are groupings "*de fait*", open rather than closed, non-assembled, permanent, remain at the bottom unorganized, and possess only conditional restraint.

The social classes are exceedingly complex and are of major importance as social frameworks for the study of the multiple manifestations of social time and their hierarchized time scales. More ostensibly than any other partial collective unity, each class possesses its own dynamic and its own time scale. This is because each is incompatible with the other classes and resists penetration by the global society to which it belongs. A class, being rebellious to the hierarchy of functional groupings which characterize the structure of the society in which it is integrated, also rejects the official time scale. A class not in power struggles to get there and moves during this struggle in its own scale of time. If a class is shorn of its power, it strives to keep intact within its own orb, as far as possible, "the good old days". If a class is destined to disappear, it is because it is a victim of a situation in which its own scale of time is entirely outmoded. In a class structure, together with class consciousness, cultural works and world view, different systems of knowledge, morality, law values etc. are class characteristics; they participate in the production of the time scale in which a class lives. Each class is a whole world unto itself and aspires to become a unique world. It identifies itself with the existing global society from which the other classes would be more or less excluded or at least placed in a subordinate position, or it identifies itself with a future global society in which there is a completely new relationship between the classes or the class divisions themselves disappear. For finally, a class may identify itself with a former global society in which this class played a dominant or at least an important role. Much more than the groupings which are at play within it, and even more than the global structure of which it is a part, every social class is characterized by a particularity and uniqueness, a historicity, so to speak, because of its relation to a specific conjuncture, to an entire "historical situation".

One is able, therefore, to postulate very little concerning the time of social classes in general, since their *raison d'être* is precisely in their opposition or even antagonism to other classes. All that can be stated is that the time scales vary from class to class. The time scales of the classes, including those which are not in power, are in opposition to the time scale of the global society. One essential characteristic is the role played by deceptive time, the time of surprise, in the time scales of all the social classes. As we have already mentioned, this social time often hides the virtual sudden and unexpected crisis, irregular pulsation and sudden leaps forward under the appearance of slowed down, long duration.

But this surprise time can manifest itself also in the opposite way with delayed time concealed under the appearance of advance, as was the case of the bourgeois class in the recent past. Today at the mid-point of the twentieth century, the working class furnishes an example of deceptive time in reverse. This is as true in the collectivistic societies as in the bourgeois regimes.

There is a two-fold explanation for the role of deceptive time in the time scale characteristic of the social classes, apart from the influence of historical conjunctures: (1) Even when the social classes are organized they never express themselves in a single organization, but always in a plurality of different organizations such as political parties, labor unions, cooperatives, mutuals, educational and athletic associations which at times compete with each other. This is particularly characteristic of the working class, partially true for the bourgeoisie, less true for the peasant class. (2) A multiplicity of different social groupings, each producing their own times, are comprised in the social classes. From this perspective, the diverse groupings within the social classes such as the family, age groupings, groupings of particular economic strata, professional groupings, and local groupings, etc. along with their times enter into these tensions and struggles of varying degrees of intensity and actuality. Within the different classes, taking into account their structures and the various partial and global conjunctures, these groupings have different hierarchized arrangements which modify the time scales of the social classes. Within this hierarchy of groupings the most important roles might go to the political parties, or to the labor unions, or the economic strata of unequal salaries and income, or they might go to the professions, the families, "active minorities", the "elites", etc. The time scales of a class can be altered in as many ways as there are different possible combinations of groupings.

This explains the striking accentuation of deceptive time or time of surprise in the life of the social classes.

Marx made the error of contrasting the social classes with only two kinds of particular groupings: the State and political parties. These are generally presented by the Marxist analysis as instruments of the class struggle in modern societies. In this way the macrocosm of groupings within the social classes is partially neglected. However, Marx was rather attentive to the heterogeneous tendencies of factions within a class, such as the industrial, financial and commercial groups within the bourgeois class[1].

At present, non-marxist analysis errs because of a different orientation. It reduces the new groupings in a social class to the strata or levels with disparity in salaries or income, needs and satisfaction of these needs. In this way the macrocosm of groupings participating in a class and the variety of criteria for the hierarchy of these groupings according to classes and conjunctures, are both extremely impoverished. In addition the very existence of social classes is practically denied by this kind of analysis. Because erratic time is peculiar to the economic strata, in so far as they effectively constitute a group, which is not always the case, no one precise time scale emerges. In fact, their variety is occasionally concealed in the different social classes. The problem which we are trying to examine here is simply evaded in the non-marxist approach.

THE PEASANT CLASS AND ITS SCALES OF SOCIAL TIME

The peasant class must not be confused with rural population. With the exception of the great landed gentry (the gentlemen farmers of yesteryear), the rural population of France seems actually to be divided into several rural classes which are in the process of formation. Does a peasant class still exist in France? Definitely its political position was elevated under the Third Republic to such an extent we may ask if it has not ceased at this moment to be a class? Moreover, the situation is not the same in other countries and particularly in other social structures. The peasant class does not exist in Great Britain or in the United States. From all evidence it would seem that in certain collectivistic countries

[1] See 'La sociologie de Karl Marx' in *La vocation actuelle de la sociologie*, Vol. II, 2nd ed., 1963, Chapter XII, pp. 267 ff. and 290 ff.

which supposedly abolished social classes as for example in the U.S.S.R., China, Jugoslavia, and Poland, the peasant class shows such a remarkable capacity to survive that it plays an important role in the evolution of these regimes.

The peasant class, after the fashion of all classes, takes on a particular definitiveness when it demonstrates its imperviousness to the global society and its opposition to the bourgeois and proletarian classes. Also, since the beginning of the seventeenth century and the birth of capitalism it is more permissible to characterize the peasantry as a specific class with its own time scale.

It is not the form of agrarian property ownership that characterizes the peasant class. The members of this class can be tenants, share croppers, farmers, or land-holders. They can be co-owners, as in the "Mir" of Russia or the "Zadruga" of Jugoslavia; members of farm cooperatives, be they voluntary or compulsory, such as the *kolkhoses*; participants in larger and more centralized enterprises, such as the *sovkhoses*. They can exploit the land either individually or collectively or as families. In all these cases, they remain representatives of the peasant class.

This class is defined, therefore, according to the following criteria: its members work the land themselves, they control a limited amount of terrain; they have class consciousness and a particular ideology. The class consciousness of the peasant is characterized by a reserve towards the city and its commotion; a suspicion of the State; a view that the major portion of State expenditures are unproductive. The peasant resents the other classes: considers the proletariat to be degraded peasants, incompetent and spendthrift; the bourgeoisie as "exploiters of the peasants" because of the high prices of industrial goods; merchants of food products and the other middlemen are even more intensely disliked. In the collectivistic regimes the bourgeoisie is replaced in the mind of the peasant by the techno-bureaucrats, particularly the official planners, even more so by the representatives of government, and "city slickers" are included in this list.

Three social times are found to be most important for the peasant class: the enduring time of long duration and slow motion, retarded time turned in on itself, and cyclical time. Added to this is deceptive time (as it is for all the social classes) and finally, time alternating between delay and advance. Erratic time, time in advance of itself, and explosive time normally do not play a role in the time scale produced by the peasant class.

An outline of the hierarchical scale of these times would be as follows:

1. Enduring time of long duration and slow motion.
2. Cyclical time related to the seasons.
3. Retarded time turned in on itself.
4. Deceptive time.
5. Time alternating between advance and delay.

Among the depth levels characteristic of the peasant class, the ecological-geographic-demographic base is strongly accentuated. The cycles of seasons and climate produce a special peasant calendar with regional variations and in which the cyclical time of nature and enduring time are reinforced. This class tends to remain faithful to traditional patterns and symbols which supports the peasants' inclination to move in retarded time turned in on itself, because traditional patterns and symbols unfold within this time. But even though agricultural techniques changed slowly before the introduction of the tractor, they changed nevertheless. This modernization was realized, and it is always realized, under the cover of deceptive time permitting interference of alternating time and erratic time. The hierarchy of times which we have just outlined is reaffirmed, first by the tendency of the peasant class to actualize community sociability, especially passive and even unconscious community, often bordering on mass sociability. Secondly, either the family, which usually takes the form of the extended family, or co-operative associations of property owners involved in a common enterprise predominates in the hierarchy of groupings. It is true that economic stratification intervenes also, but the rich peasants give pre-eminence to the extended family and stratification only affects the peasant class time scale when it is close to dissolving.

Only religious and civil wars, political, social or technical revolutions, international wars and epidemics can jolt the peasant class time. At certain historical conjunctures the time scale of the peasant class can even play an active role in great social upheavals. This is clearly evident in the French, Russian and Chinese revolutions, in the Napoleonic wars, the *coup d'état* by Louis Bonaparte or during the two World Wars. Only then do erratic time and time in advance of itself take first place in the hierarchy, upsetting the customary time scale of the peasant class. But this never lasts long as their exigencies and aspirations are always somewhat limited. Once satisfied this class turns in on itself and continues to live according to its characteristic scale of time, even if the most modern techniques are put at its disposal as in the U.S.S.R. and China today. The other possibility is the disintegration of the peasant class and the formation of new rural classes. This turn of events is being experienced in several occidental countries today.

Is the peasant class aware of its scale of time and does it seek to master it? It would seem that the response is in the affirmative. Where the peasant class exists, perception, symbolization, conceptualization and measurement of time enters into its class consciousness. The local folk festivals and regional seasonal calendars give evidence to this fact. Moreover, to the degree that the peasant class opposes the other classes and the global society, it affirms, tries to maintain and command its own social time scale. Thus it seeks to master its manifestations of social time, ultimately resisting the harassing and anxious times of the bourgeoisie, the proletariat and the techno-bureaucracy. The former two classes are locked in a constant struggle for domination over industrial society. Unlike the State and the church, the peasant class does not attempt to force its specific scale of time on everyone else. Its attitude is that of retreat and passive resistance, since it is convinced that each class has its own time and time scales which it merits.

THE BOURGEOIS CLASS AND ITS SCALES OF SOCIAL TIME

Since the beginning of capitalism and up to the twentieth century the bourgeois class has been of major importance in our societies. It has held uncontested power in the industrial societies. In some cases, as in England after the British revolution, and in France after the French revolution, the bourgeoisie held this power in coalition with other classes. According to particular periods and conjunctures first it played the role of a revolutionary *avant-garde*, later became moderate, conservative and finally reactionary. Also, it is sometimes pacifist, sometimes war-mongering, sometimes nationalistic and sometimes international, according to the particular circumstances and their own interests.

Ownership of the means of production, the source of raw materials and financial capital plus control of the market have always played a primary role in the formation of the bourgeois class. Even so, this class has been able to integrate all the economically prosperous strata of the society including the liberal professions, the technical and administrative managers in the bureaucracies which it actually created as well as the high-level functionaries of the State into a tentative unity. The bourgeois class has never been limited solely to industrial magnates or to employers. The many groupings of this class are arranged in a hierarchy according to income and wealth, the criteria important for the economic strata. As revealed in Marx this hierarchy of strata runs up against a latent conflict among the three factions of the bourgeoisie: the industrial, the financial bourgeoisie and the commercial bourgeoisie, to whom managers are being more and more closely linked. The managers, much more than all the other factions of the bourgeoisie, are demonstrating their capacity to survive in collectivistic States, even while the disintegration and elimination of the bourgeois class takes place. Even more, they tend to dominate the other factions of the bourgeois class in fully developed organized capitalist societies, e.g. United States, Great Britain and West-Germany.

Thus far, we have called attention to the fact that the bourgeois class was largely open to all prosperous groupings and that it included, along with high-level financiers and businessmen, the liberal professions, high-level functionaries, plus technical and administrative managers of industry. This class also encompasses bankers, as well as corporations formed by trusts and cartels. The bourgeois class is much more inclined than the other classes, to establish a hierarchy of groupings according to the predominant criteria of the economic strata, wealth and income. During the nineteenth century, the period of growth for this class, the "captains of industry" who were good organizers and calculators, clairvoyant entrepreneurs, generous and philanthropic men, were also the representatives of the most fortunate stratum of the bourgeoisie. The bourgeois class, linked more than all the other social classes to immediate economic success and a prosperity welded to business enterprise, possessed a class consciousness characterized by confidence in an unlimited "technical and economic progress", confidence in the harmony of the interests of all, in the universal benefits of capitalism and urban culture. In direct contrast to the class consciousness of the peasant class which turns in on itself, the bourgeois class consciousness lends itself to universal diffusion, to penetration into very diverse milieux.

Even the idea of progress, above all an automatic progress accom-

93

plished with a minimum of struggle and upheaval by the single force of development of technical means and soaring prosperity, is essentially a part of bourgeois ideology. Widespread economic crisis, limitations of the market, the labor movement, the reduction of the margin of profit closely tied to larger and larger investments, the many conflicts between the self-interests of the bourgeoisie and the application of newer and newer technical means (Marx has already pointed out all these elements) have not yet succeeded in eradicating the optimistic and universal base of bourgeois ideology, at times diminished but always persisting.

Therefore the bourgeois class emphasizes time alternating between advance and delay, deceptive time, time where advance and delay are in desperate conflict and erratic time. Time turned in on itself has the least importance. In spite of the opposite impression, time in advance as well as the explosive time of creation intervene only in exceptional conjunctures.

We can therefore outline the hierarchy of social times in which the bourgeois class tends to move:

1. Time alternating between advance and delay.
2. Deceptive time where delay is concealed in an apparent advance.
3. A time where advance and delay are in sharp struggle.
4. Erratic time.
5. The delayed time turned in on itself.

The amazing thing to note is that the bourgeois class does not produce the time scale expected in light of its orientation. The destiny of the bourgeois class, linked as it is with private ownership of the means of production, liquid assets, economic success and a prosperous situation, so often delays technological change and economic reorganization that its forward momentum is very limited.

Instead of time leaping forward, we find time alternating between advance and delay in first position. This is because the bourgeois class has always had to defend its economic acquisitions, protect its privileged, prosperous status and its property. This was true even when it was only a rising class which had not as yet taken power and incarnated the aspirations of the whole society. The scale of social time produced by the bourgeoisie creates the illusion that time leaping forward predominates, not only because of the bourgeois ideology of progress, but also because of the relative rapidity of cadence, rhythm and mobility of this class. However, this rapid rhythm is not that of movement towards the future but of alternation between advance and delay. How could it be otherwise, if one keeps in mind that the bourgeois class must, in order to persist, partially subordinate the proletarian and peasant classes? Thus it is that time alternating between advance and delay is joined with deceptive time. This, rather than being advance camouflaged by delay, is on the contrary, retarded time masked by advance. If there is any advance, it is realized only for a narrow, privileged stratum. The other classes have to wait patiently for a long period of time for the questionable benefits of this advance. Elsewhere, while glorifying the latest technical inventions, the bourgeois class guards them well, preventing their application when it would require going beyond a certain margin of investments calculated and guaranteed as profitable. Moreover, economic crises and competition, whether the competition is individual or collective, between trusts and cartels, between nations or different regimes can force the hand of the bourgeois class. We are, therefore, in the presence of a merciless, unrelenting struggle between the time in advance and retarded time and it is not a matter of time merely alternating. The more the bourgeois class feels its very existence menaced by the rising collectivist regimes (centralized or decentralized), or, by the promotion in its own midst of the managerial group preparing itself to become a class, the more it has tended to favor delayed time turned in on itself, clinging to exhausted or anachronistic political regimes and to organizational methods and technology on the way to being outmoded. The other perspective is the possibility of orientation of this class toward fascist regime and alliance with technocracy.[1]

All this does not impede the bourgeois class from playing an *avant garde* role in political revolutions and counter-revolutions which turn out to be to its own profit, nor of becoming in certain conjunctures one of the main forces of colonial, international and sometimes even civil wars. It is then, but then only, that time in advance of itself, linked ordinarily to erratic time comes to the surface within the bourgeois class. However, it is very rare that these two times are combined with explosive time of creation.

The bourgeois class remains, therefore, a prudent agent even at the height of great turmoil. It has too much to lose in any sort of crisis, and most important of all, its very existence is always threatened in these

[1] See pp. 142–144.

circumstances. Favoring mostly compromise, inclined to make certain concessions, it very easily becomes very moderate or conservative as long as its economic interests are not gravely menaced.

The bourgeois class, ordinarily tends to limit the awareness and perception of its own time and of its scale of time to economic activities and to conceptualize them through the intermediary of size of investments, price of merchandise, frequency of movements of goods, and the importance of profits.

The bourgeois awareness of time is very well expressed in the saying, "time is money". It favors the spontaneous quantification of time, but has confidence in the quantification of that State and global society in which it dominates. This tendency towards using the general standards for the quantification of time is reinforced by its inclination to consider its own scale of time as universal. The effort to master its time is expressed in the organization of production so as to increase its productivity and reduce costs. One could therefore, say that the bourgeois class does not struggle especially to maintain its own scale of time, but rather that the problem of time is only related to economic production and profit.

THE PROLETARIAN SOCIAL TIME SCALE

The working class or the proletariat which occupies a non-privileged place in industry because it does not own productive property and only lives from its labor, whether skilled or unskilled or prepared by professional training, has been slow to organize and develop class consciousness. This is due in part to the heterogeneous origin of the working class, who was recruited from the poor population of the cities, the bankrupted artisans and from the lower levels of the peasantry. The class consciousness of the proletariat only dates back to the beginning of the nineteenth century and was manifested in the various socialist and collectivist ideologies, including Marxism which became the dominant expression in a later period. Nevertheless, neither the different interpretations of Marxism nor any other doctrine has been able to substitute for the proletarian consciousness itself. This is a much richer, more complex and more fluctuating phenomenon than any single doctrine, ideology, idea or spontaneous reaction. This consciousness includes among other things the awareness of needs, aspirations of the future, the collective memory of dramatic historical events such as the insurrection of 1848, the *Commune*, the *Popular Front*, of political and labor union struggles, the resistance during the war, the consciousness of successively suffered deceptions, etc. The hierarchy of groupings constituting the working class, in contrast to that of the bourgeois class, is not based primarily on economic strata, such as electrical workers and printers – the highest paid – on the one side, long-shoremen and porters – the poorest paid – on the other side, nor on occupational training. Instead, this hierarchy is based on the role of certain groups in the class struggle, that is by labor union elites, worker delegates, active minorities. Yet, this tendency is not manifested with the same clarity in every conjuncture.

The workers can enter into conflict with their own organizations and feel crushed and betrayed by the new bureaucracy which directs them. Even more seriously, the working class, in a fully collectivistic regime, can feel exploited by the State which promised to it power and can find itself dominated by the new techno-bureaucratic class whose influence and authority could not be circumvented.

The class consciousness of the proletarist can therefore be harassed, divided, ambivalent and torn by internal struggles. It can withdraw within itself in an indifferent and prolonged apathy. It would, therefore, be erroneous to represent the proletarian class as uniquely revolutionary, destructive of the bourgeois regime and of all exploitation of man by man, or as creator of regimes which realize all of the proletarian aspirations.

The effective role of the proletariat, as well as its destiny, its consciousness and its situation are not as simple or as univocal as Marx believed. The twentieth century has shown this very well. We can only presuppose that sooner or later the worker self-management of industry in connection with decentralized collectivist planning will cause the working class to emerge from the inferior position in which it finds itself for different reasons in capitalism and even in the centralized, collectivistic regimes.

Keeping in mind this complex situation, we now shall analyze the variations of the social time scale belonging to the proletarian class and present a simplified and general scheme of it. In this scale time in advance of itself and explosive time, the first projecting the future into the present and the second obliterating the present and the past in the creation of the future, are the generally emphasized times. Yet, the time in advance of itself to which we refer here, is only a time of profoundly uncertain aspirations. Explosive time blurring as it does, the present and the past is only the project time of the permanent revolution. In the face of the real facts, it has seldom an effective duration. Finally, the most effective, appear to be erratic time and deceptive time, in which the time in advance is hidden under the time of delay and the time of delay under the time of advance. Next the time of struggle between advance and delay and the time alternating between the two.

Therefore, the social time scale in which the proletarian class evolves could be outlined as follows:

1. The time ahead of itself.
2. Explosive time.
3. Erratic time.
4. Deceptive time in the two senses.
5. The time of struggle between advance and delay.
6. The time alternating between precipitation and slowing down.
7. Cyclical time and the time of slowed down, long duration are relegated to last place.

Of all the classes, the proletariat produces the richest, the most diverse and also the most variable scale of time because any one of the following variables could radically change this time scale. It depends on whether the mass sociability or the communion sociability, either passive or active, are accentuated; whether labor unions or political groups predominate in its hierarchy of groupings; whether organizations are united or divided; whether the leadership directing worker organizations is used up or not; whether the family or economic strata take on an unexpected importance, which is the first sign of fatigue and apathy in this class; whether the working class permits a centralized, collectivistic State to dominate it temporarily; whether the proletariat struggles alone or is allied with other classes. In sum, any one of these variables can basically change the social time scale which is produced by the proletarian class. This does not exclude the possibility that under other conditions the time scale could be oriented towards the current demiurgical image.

These variations in the time scale of the working class do not depend on the number of proletarians. For example, the workers constitute 70 per cent of the English and German population, whereas this proportion drops to about 50 per cent in France and to 40 per cent in U.S.S.R.

As long as the working class remains the greatest revolutionary force in our societies, a time scale where the predominant influence is held by time ahead of itself, explosive time and erratic time becomes very effective at certain propitious conjunctures. But revolution can not be permanent. Hence, the time ahead of itself moving in the direction of explosive time would only last in a planned economy, directed and controlled by the workers themselves.

To what degree does the proletarian class exhibit a consciousness of its time and scales of time? In what manner does it seek to master its own time? The consciousness of time of the working class often takes the form of fatigue, expectation, or hope. Its strongly emotional coloration culminates in utopias and "social myths", as the term is used by Sorel.[1]

This consciousness of time is highly symbolic and does not include any quantification. If a decentralized collectivism in which the workers actively participate in management and planning would be realized, and if in this structure the proletarian class would continue to assert itself as such, it is very likely that its consciousness of time would be modified profoundly and would become more rational.

As far as the mastery of time is concerned, it is only during periods of revolution that the proletariat appears to control its time and its scale of time. Yet this is more a matter of the awareness of this mastery rather than the effective control of time. It is only in controlling the economic planning through democratic self-government that the working class would be able to reach the point of real mastery of its time and its scale of time.

THE MIDDLE CLASSES AND THE TECHNO-BUREAUCRATS; THEIR SOCIAL TIME SCALES

It is common practice to speak of the middle classes in the plural rather than of the middle class in the singular. This is because a multiplicity of collectivities exist which do not succeed in finding their place between the working class and the bourgeois class. It is not only a matter of the "petit bourgeoisie" of Karl Marx, such as artisans and small business men who are far from disappearing. In fact technical development and professional

---

[1] Gurvitch refers to the French syndicalist thinker and philosopher, Georges Sorel (1847–1922). Sorel declared that "social myths" are essential for every revolutionary movement. They give unity and purpose to the rising class (P.B.).

redistributions could cause them to have a resurgence of life. It is equally a matter of an army of employees, officials who are paid an average wage, middlemen of different kinds and self-employed workers. Normally, these diverse groups are not structured in a special class; they do not have "class consciousness" as do the bourgeoisie and the proletariat. But, as much as they are aware of their situation they have an ambiguous, ambivalent, broken and tenuous consciousness of their class. In the conflict of classes they can go in one direction or another, or occupy a position quite apart. In France, the middle classes were able to support the radical-socialist party during the best days of the Third Republic, whereas the middle classes in Italy and Germany favored fascist regimes after the war of 1914–1918. They are extremely divided in France after the Second World War and numerous splinter groups developed. In England, where they play a far less important role, they have been drawn to the workers' party or the liberals. In the United States and present day France they have become partisans of conservatism of different degrees. In the majority of cases the so-called "middle classes" do not constitute real social classes, although in certain situations they could very likely become such a class.

It seems clear that these intermediate groups do not produce their own time scales. They are tossed between diverse social times and are unsuccessful in finding even a tenuous cohesion between these times. The middle classes are harrassed by the chaos of social times in which they live. They are prey to perpetual fear of the social times confronting them. In this situation erratic time functions most effectively. These groupings would reach beyond this erratic time and free themselves from their servitude to the chaotic social times only if they succeeded in integrating themselves into an effective social class. In sum, there are no other collectivities which are less able to master their time, less susceptible even to grasping their own social times, than the groups which are designated as "middle classes".

The virtual class of managers[1] formed in organized Capitalism represents only a fraction of the bourgeois class. But in fascist regimes this latent class soon illustrated that it was capable of challenging the very existence of the bourgeois class and even supplanting it. It showed moreover, a particular aptitude to survive and to adapt to the social revolutions which

[1] See *La vocation actuelle de la sociologie*, Vol. II, 2nd ed., 1963, pp. 431–461.

create centralized, collectivistic structures. The force of the techno-bureaucrats resides in their exceptional technical competence, organizing and administrative ability; even more, in their omni-presence which extends all the way from large business concerns such as trusts and cartels, to political machines, labor unions, employer associations; from top-level State administrations to economic planning agencies and international associations, to the major divisions of modern armies. The more technical skills advance by leaps and bounds, the more the administration of large organized bodies gains in importance without finding a counterpart in the development of new forms of control by those submitted to such volunteered leadership. The more the techno-bureaucrats became powerful, the more they try to organize themselves into a social class marching towards power.

One of the weaknesses of the techno-bureaucrats lies in the possible conflict of interests which could take place between the diverse groups of the technicians-experts, administrators, organizers and planners, who thus face a latent conflict among themselves and with the high level military men. Their second weakness comes from the fact that the techno-bureaucrats have even greater difficulty asserting themselves as a social class since their different groups do not live in the same social time. In their diverse milieus strong barriers are placed in the way of establishing one unique scale of social time. Thus, the economic planners live in a time ahead of itself, which, at the slightest error and in the face of every unforeseen obstacle, is reversed, and becomes a time behind itself. The technical experts live in a time alternating between advance and delay. Though this alternation is precipitated by the rapidity of technical discoveries, it remains an alternation with all of these uncertainties. The organizers and industrial engineers, live in a time, sometimes in advance, sometimes behind itself, combined with the time of surprise where continuity plays hide and seek with the constant possibility of sudden crises. Public service bureaucrats are often encased in a time of slowed down, long duration. The time of military logistic experts, like that of all technical experts, is a time of alternation. It is powerfully limited by the time of long duration arising from demographic considerations and by erratic time arising from the political, economic and financial uncertainties and from their own intrigues.

This diversity of social times is one of the reasons the "class consciousness" of the technocrats has not been too effective, even if it is expressed in an ideology proclaiming a superhuman "competence of elites", where the simple mortal is transformed into a tool or an extension of a tool. The techno-bureaucratic groupings are victims of an illusion: they imagine themselves living in a time ahead of itself or even in an explosive time of creation which they think they alone know how to dominate. In reality, they do not succeed, either in a clear consciousness of the effective times in which they live, or in unifying real times into a scale, or being able to master such a time scale. The worst is that they draw the societies where they prepare to seize power towards the risk of being carried away, if not annihilated, by the engines and their forces moving in times which no class nor human force can dominate or arrest.

CHAPTER VII

GLOBAL SOCIETIES AND THEIR TIME SCALES

The global societies comprise specific total social phenomena. They are at one and the same time the largest, the most imposing, the richest in content and the most influential in a given social reality. They go beyond not only the functional groupings and the social classes but even their various conflicting hierarchies, in plenitude and authority. These "macrocosms of social macrocosms" possess a juridical sovereignty which delimits the powers of all groupings including the State competing with them. The juridical sovereignty of the State has never ceased to be relative and subordinate to the global society despite all appearance of the contrary. The global societies also possess a certain social sovereignty over all the social collectivities which are part of them; as a matter of fact they play the leading role. A global society is not only structurable, but always actually structured and usually organizations enter into its structure. But the structures, whether global or partial, and the multiple organizations, never express the total social global phenomenon, not only, because it is supra-functional *par excellence*, but even more because it is the most mobile and the richest of all microsocial and macrosocial substructures.

In other words, there is always more movement back and forth in the total global social phenomenon than in its global structure. The global structure tends to be more stable than the partial structures. A social structure and especially a global social structure can maintain its precarious equilibrium only by a constant effort of repeated structuration to combat the movement of destructuration and avoid the bursting of the structure. Independent of this fact, there is also a very marked divergency between the movement of the global structure and the movement of the subjacent total social phenomenon. The movement of the global social phenomenon constantly spills over in its ebb and flow onto the movement of its structure and thereby is a persistent menace to it. This produces repercussions which affect the relationships between the time scale characteristic of a global structure and the time scale produced by the total social phenomenon which is subjacent to it. We are confronted here by two scales of

103

time: (1) more firmly hierarchized and unified in the global social structure; (2) more flexible, more tenuous and active in the global societies themselves. It is impossible to reduce this dual scale of time to long or short duration; to the past, present or future; to continuity or discontinuity; to the quantitive or qualitative. These two scales of time can enter in different combinations. Thus an inclusive society and its structure have always two hierarchies of time which can be partially analogous but never identical. Often they are in conflict with each other.

It is impossible to establish types of global societies without starting by analysis of their structure. But there is always a leap to be made in order to reach beyond the type of structure to the type of total social phenomenon itself. The social structures require, in order to be classified into types, that the following criteria be applied: (1) the hierarchy of groupings, (2) the probable combination of the manifestations of sociability, (3) the tendency to actualize particular depth levels of social reality, (4) the scale of modes of division of labor and accumulation, (5) the hierarchy of social regulations or social controls, (6) the systems of cultural works constituting the civilization, and (7) the scale of social times. This seventh aspect will be specially stressed here by the study of its correlation to the global social structure. This quasi-official scale of social times characteristic for the social structure is often overcome by the time scale corresponding to the total social phenomenon.

The matter of the total social phenomenon invading with its global time scale the precarious equilibrium of the global structure poses some particularly delicate problems for the different types of so-called prehistorical societies. Modern ethnologists and ethnographers attribute too great an importance to the most minute details of the archaic structures and to the "unconscious" and "subconscious" characteristics of the totalities which are subjacent to them. This illustrates the difficulty peculiar to an approach that moves from the structure to penetrate in the total social phenomenon itself when the latter is completely strange to the observer. It would be as false to reduce all of the archaic societies to a single type or to some aspects of a single type as it would be to multiply them *ad infinitum*, thus substituting geographic ethnography for sociology.

We shall only present therefore, the four types of archaic structures and societies which we distinguished in our book *Détermi-*

nismes sociaux et liberté humaine (1955, 2nd. ed. 1963). Admittedly, it would be possible and even desirable to go further. The question which interests us is what repercussions they have on the social time scales. Next, several types of "civilized" or *historical societies* will be delineated. However, it seems more precise to label the latter *promethean societies* because of the promethean element in the collective and individual consciousness of the human freedom which intervene here actively and effectively in social life. This intervention can result in change, restructure, or even split and destructure of the global society. An ostensible and conscious struggle between tradition, reform and revolution is manifested in these "historical" societies; this dialectic assures the transmitted or rediscovered ties with our own society. Nevertheless, these historical societies will be studied *sociologically* generalizing them as far as possible into qualitative, discontinuous types, rather than historically, singularizing and distinguishing each one from the other and searching for continuity in their change.

THE TIME SCALES OF ARCHAIC[1] SOCIETIES

The four types of so-called archaic structures and societies are: (1) Tribal societies, where clans predominate but family bands compete with them. Such types are found, or have been found, among the Indians of South America and in certain regions of Australia. (2) Societies where the tribes integrate varied and slightly hierarchized groupings: clan, magical, familial, local, military, professional, etc. Their cohesion consists in their submission to a chief with mythological power. Ethnographers such as Malinowski, Williamson, Lehmann and Maurice Leenhardt have repeatedly discovered varied examples of this type in Polynesia as well as in Melanesia, existing side by side with other types of archaic societies. (3) Organized tribal societies with military divisions, extended and domestic families, where the clans are scarcely observable. The American ethnographers, Boas, Lowie, Eggan, Hoebel and others as well as the French, Mauss and Davy, both followers of Durkheim, have found examples of these societies in the extreme northwest of the United States, such as the

---

[1] G. Gurvitch prefers the term "archaic" to "primitive"; archaic societies are "not promethean". See *Déterminismes sociaux et liberté humaine*, 2nd ed., 1963, pp. 220–221. (Tr.)

Cherokee and the Kwakiutl. (4) Organized monarchic tribal societies which partially retain their clan divisions, but in which local groupings predominate over a series of other groupings. These are sustained by a theogonic and cosmogonic mythology which enters directly into the functioning of the social structure. Evans Pritchard and Fortes, Herskovits, Baumann, Westermann, Tempels, Griaule, Radcliffe-Brown and Dariell Forde have studied certain archaic structures of Negro Africa which are partially or entirely of this type. However, this is only one among many types of global structures that can be observed in Africa.

These four types of archaic structures and societies will not be analyzed separately but the fact that the scales of social time are different in each type must be underlined. These different time scales exist in spite of the presence of a specific "mythological time" which goes back to the "origins" and in which the religion, the nature and the social life become identical. These origins are placed as much in the present as in the past and the future, which are not clearly distinguished and are joined together in a kind of "eternal recurring" cycle. Sometimes mythological time is superimposed on enduring and slowed down time, combined with erratic time arising from surprises which push the floundering embryonic organization through schisms and wars. Sometimes the mythological time is allied to magical time linked to "Mana". This alliance leans on the efforts of groups and individuals and is manifested in exchanges, in the circulation of goods and persons. All this tends to give to mythological-magical time, the appearance at least of the time leaping forward in spite of its propensity towards cyclical time. However, even when time pushing forward succeeds in breaking through effectively, its push is often stopped by the resistance of crystallized patterns and symbols. Thus retarded time combined with enduring time regularly triumphs in the end over the time leaping forward and even over alternating time.

But it happens that mythological time is forcefully limited by the pantheistic character of the religious beliefs which obliterate all distinction between transcendent supernatural forces and immanent magical, supernatural forces. Then the social time in which social roles, competitive relationships and even rudimentary organizations evolve is accentuated. This is a deceptive time, where time leaping forward and sudden crises are hidden behind delay and where erratic time seems to play a more influential role than would be expected. Under certain favorable conditions, this situation leads these social structures and global societies to produce organizations of extremely vast size. The empire of the Incas is direct proof of this. Finally, as illustrated in the great Negro monarchies, mythological and cyclical time can in some cases serve also time leaping forward. This is manifested in the movement for expansion. Hence here, the appropriate symbols and rites, far from moving in retarded time seem rather to participate in the production of new symbolic contents, thus encouraging time leaping forward. Elsewhere erratic time and the time alternating between advance and delay play far more important roles here than deceptive time. This social time scale remains ambivalent, for even while its inclination toward precipitation serves time pushing forward, it is arrested by the time of slowed down long duration of the ecological base and by the mythological and cyclical times. In these four types of archaic societies it is evidently impossible for an outside observer to penetrate in the scales of time characteristic of the subjacent total social phenomena, even though starting from the semi-official time of the structure.

It is equally difficult to say if the diverse archaic societies are conscious of the time otherwise than by myths, rites, ages of man, seasons, exchanges and expansion. In any case one can at least state categorically that the different types of archaic societies and structures do not master their time scale. Myths here are more than likely efforts of these societies to rid themselves of the time-conflicts, than they are attempts to dominate them. It is totally different for the historic societies which we suggest to be called promethean.

THE TYPES OF HISTORICAL SOCIETIES

Types of promethean global societies or historical societies can be distinguished by starting with their structures, and by arriving at the total global social phenomena themselves. They are as follows:
1. Charismatic theocracies.
2. Patriarchal Societies.
3. Feudal societies.
4. Global societies where the City-States predominate. They are usually in the process of becoming Empires.
5. Societies of nascent capitalism and so-called' 'enlightened" absolutism.

6. Democratic-liberal global societies with competitive capitalism.
There are four global societies competing today:
7. Societies with fully developed and organized capitalism.
8. Fascist societies with a techno-bureaucratic base.
9. Planned societies based on State collectivism.
10. Planned societies based on pluralistic decentralized collectivism.

CHARISMATIC THEOCRACIES AND THEIR SOCIAL TIME SCALES

Global Societies of this type are only relatively homogeneous. Its uni-fication, although difficult, results from the fact that the State and the Church are identified in a single, pre-eminent organization which finds its supreme incarnation in a King-Priest-Living God. The power of the dynasties and their representatives is supernatural and at the same time charismatically personal. There are diverse examples such as Babylonia, Assyria, the Hittite kingdom, Egypt, Persia, Ancient China and Japan, Tibet, India. The Khalifat of Islam under the dynasties of the Ammeyades and the Abbassides of the eighth through the twelfth centuries is a special form of the charismatic theocracy. Also, it is possible to mention the Inca Empire of Peru.

The structures of these societies are characterized by the following traits: (1) The State-Church predominates over the other groupings. Certain groupings such as the patriarchal family in China and Japan, the priestly castes in Egypt and India, military groupings and at a lower level the professional fraternities of merchants and artisans are very active. (2) Masses predominate over Community and Communion. Communions are limited to the groupings of priests and the initiates of special cults. (3) There is an accentuation first, on organizations of extremely vast scope; second, a particular emphasis on the ecological base; third, on beliefs, religious and mystic symbols, along with a myth system. (4) The division of technical labor is often very developed and certain techniques such as those of the embalmers in Egypt and the carvers in China are highly elaborated. (5) In the hierarchy of social control the predominant positions of such social regulations as religion, magic and myths is unexpectedly contested by traditional morality, imperative morality, technical knowledge, secular law and art, limiting the power of religon and magic. (6) In the system of cultural works, the mystical side of the structure clings to the surface rather than penetrating to a more profound level.

Moreover, these last traits are true for this global structure in its entirety. The theocracy is here only an official useful screen. What takes place, under cover of the theocratic-charismatic structure, really represents only an official and very limited aspect. The life of the total social phenomena of these global societies is much richer and much more active than appears at first glance. All that we know about these societies is that extensive levels of social reality are developed in connection with rationalism, economic calculation, exchanges, the individual law of obligation, contract, pledge, credit and the proliferation of special, secular groupings, such as professional groupings or craft guilds in Egypt and the merchant societies in the Khalifats. In addition, large heterogeneous masses of conquered people and slaves are agitated. Life within the theocratic-charismatic structures is not calm as one would logically expect. It explodes at different turning points and undergoes revolutions, a proof of the intense invasion by its subjacent total phenomena.

In sum, the theocratic-charismatic global social structure diverges clearly from the total global phenomenon of this society. The structure appears as a screen behind which the much more complex and agitated total phenomenon is concealed.

Before we deal with the scale of social times in the official structure of the charismatic theocracies, we raise the question, "Can one speak of time here so far as the last was defined as a coordination or else a divergency of movements?" How can we talk of time when the pre-supposed fusion of the divine world, the social world and the world of nature to support these social structures, would in actuality lead to *immobility and eternity*? The integration of immanence in transcendence would in any case contribute to a great stability and possible mummification. But if in the charismatic-theocratic structures a definite effort is made to master the social times in "living eternity" which promises to get rid of time, it is equally clear that this effort fails. Diverse aspects of this failure can be observed. First the theogonies and cosmogonies, which are often combined with vitalistic beliefs (force and fertility) play a considerable role here within the corresponding religions. Next, the interdependence of magic and religion renders the theocratic-charismatic structures susceptible to changes and movements more than one would expect. It accentuates the preponderance of immanent supernatural forces over the transcendent supernatural ones. Finally, the charisma of the King – Priest – Living God stirs the enormous organizations over which he is the chief; he unleashes social movements even through the ceremonies, mysteries and rites. The charismatic leader finds himself, as a "first cause", caught at the same time in the chain of immanent and transcendent movements of which he is only a link.

Thus the theocratic-charismatic structure, independent of the fact that it is only an official and very thin screen, tries in vain to catalyze the turbulent forces of these societies. In doing so it is caught in diverse movements thereby presupposing a time scale within which it operates. This can be verified by the fact that it is precisely in a number of these theocratic-charismatic structures, State-Churches and Church-States, that the first conceptualizations, as well as measures of time were elaborated. Such were the calendars, the first rational scales of time. Assyria, Babylonia and above all ancient Egypt confirm this affirmation. The seasons, astral periods, the flooding of the Nile, the systems of irrigation which were tied to it and finally the holidays and religious ceremonies did help to the establishing of measures of time.

Let us return to the problem of scales of time in the official structure of the charismatic theocracies:

1. Ideologically, cyclical time of a mystic-mythological character, a time turned inward (a dance on one spot) where the past, present and future are mutually projected into each other, occupies the first place. But this time of the "eternal cycle" overflows its own boundaries, aligning itself with vitalistic and magical beliefs whose force and richness are always greater in each final stage of a cycle. Nevertheless, this time does not escape being placed at the service of the enormous organizations incarnating the State-Church.

2. However, these enormous organizations move in a deceptive time or the time of surprise. This time plays a predominant role in the charismatic-theocracies which have experienced ruptures in dynasties, conflicts between them and the priestly castes and patriarchal families, and even true revolutions. Among the best known of these revolutions are the democratization of the funeral rites, the admission of the plebians to the mysteries of the Isis-Osiris cult, the organization of the professions integrated into the State at the end of the eleventh dynasty in Egypt, the revolt

110

of the "Yellow Turbans" and the "Red Eyebrows" in Imperial China. Thus, under apparent calm and delay, deceptive time in reality masks potentiality of sudden crises.

3. This tendency towards deceptive time is reinforced in the theocratic-charismatic structure by erratic time which is characteristic of the great masses of people. Such masses were present because vast multitudes of conquered peoples and slaves were conscripted for labor on the gigantic building projects as the pyramids for example, integrated into the armies, or into the great cities populaces.

4. In contrast to these times, the time of slowed down long duration of the ecological base is assigned to fourth place.

5. Fifth place in the scale of social time is occupied by retarded time in which the mystic symbols and the economic and technical patterns dependent upon them move.

In the semi-official time-scale, the time alternating between advance and delay, the time leaping forward and explosive time have little influence.

But in this type of society we encounter dual scales of time and their conflict. For in these global societies, the total social phenomenon transcends its structure very clearly, as we have already observed and it lives according to another scale of times. We know that certain important levels of the total social phenomena developed with the rise of rationalism, economic calculation, exchange and the proliferation of special secular groups. The accentuation of intergroup and inter-personal relations with Others in all their various forms is also very evident and has repercussions on law. Its importance and unexpected expression can be observed in inter-individual law: bonds, contracts, and the whole area of credit. This law extends so far at times as to include the transfer of all property and the parcelling of the land as is illustrated in the Code of Hammurabi. As can be seen in Egypt, Babylonia, and with the Khalifats of Islam, this kind of law depends upon the juridical authority of the civil and lay tribunals functioning alongside the temple tribunals. If one adds the accumulation of fabulous riches in Egypt, China, India and among the Khalifats, which come from widespread commerce, the production of precious stones, of gold and silver, one has an image of the total global phenomenon which is quite different from that of its structure.

Hence, it will not be astonishing to see a completely different time scale arising in the subjacent society. It would look something like this:

1. In first place is the sharp struggle waged between the time leaping forward and the time behind itself. This contest is due to certain unforeseen technological changes which have been promoted by the growth of gigantic organizations. This growth, often astonishing, penetrates deeply into the economic life and leads to an emphasis on rationalism freed from mysticism in certain areas. The time of slowed down long duration at the ecological base, particularly its geographic and demographic manifestations, shares first place with the time pushing forward and time behind itself because these technological changes, organizations and rational tendencies never sufficiently succeed in overcoming the resistance of the ecological base.

2. In second position is time alternating between advance and delay which is peculiar to technical skills. New technical patterns are delayed here as they are in most societies.

3. In third rank is erratic time belonging not only to the masses, but to the intense conflictual character of these societies of such an immense size. Pulled apart by contradictory tendencies, these societies do not successfully adjust their structures and their total social phenomenon.

4. Cyclical time combined with retarded time and deceptive time, which the organizations seek in vain to master, is fourth.

5. Last place is assigned to explosive time of creation and aspiration, always latent in these societies. It is manifested directly in revolutions, changes of dynasties, through wars, in the collapse of empires and the breakdown of structures. Moreover, the ostensible competition between the two scales of time described here, gives explosive time an unexpected opportunity to operate in these societies.

In conclusion, let us note that there is an awareness of these social times and a real effort to master them, but only as related to the scales of time belonging to the semi-official structure. Here, only the enormous organizations of State-Churches are aware of time and make an effort to master it. Only the dynasties and the priestly castes grasp the social time-scale, seek to conceptualize, as well as finally to measure time through the medium of calendars. They also try do dominate the social times, to master the two competing time scales in the interests of the first. Within this first scale they seek to assure triumph of cyclical time and of deceptive time but without success. The theocratic-charismatic structures live out a perpetual drama which pervades their time scales.

THE PATRIARCHAL SOCIETIES AND THEIR SCALES OF TIME

The case for the so-called patriarchal societies is very different. Here there is a very pronounced correspondence between the structure and the total social phenomenon. Consequently, the two scales of social time show very insignificant differences.

In this type of global society, the structure is based on the exclusive pre-eminence of the largely extended domestic-familial group based on blood relationship preferably of the male filial line whether polygamous or not. This extended family absorbs all other groupings: economic, locality, neighborhood (when the society is sedentary), sex, age and mystic-ecstatic groupings. All the economic, political and religious activities are centered in the extended domestic family; the patriarch being simultaneously father, property owner, entrepreneur, priest and political leader. The domestic family is thus at the same time an economic enterprise, a State and a Church. Nevertheless, the roles of father, property owner and entrepreneur are much more accentuated than those of political leader and priest. In fact, the gods or God which the patriarch serves, are primarily family gods or domestic gods. Here, religion is entirely in the service of the family circle, and involves a radically reduced mysticism, serving rather as a kind of moralizing rational guarantee.

This observation is applicable to the type of structure which emerges from the Old Testament and that which is marked in the *Odyssey* and the *Iliad*. It is also applicable to the Roman family before its integration into the city and to the German *Hausgenossenschaft* which were associations of several patriarchs. It is interesting to note that the survivals or analogous forms of global society and global structure of this type such as the *Latifundia* of the high Roman Empire, the slavian Zadrugas, the patrimonial monarchies, such as the Frankish monarchies of the sixth to the ninth centuries, are all linked with very different kinds of religions. They include monotheism, polytheism, paganism, Judaism, and Christianity. This shows that in the life of these societies and in the equilibrium of their structure, religion tends to play only a very secondary role. This patriarchal structure is characterized among other things, by the absence of any differentiation of powers, the exceptional weakness, if not absence, of special groupings and the quasi-rational and secular atmosphere of their functioning. (*Veralltäglichung des Charismas* – Max Weber.)

113

If we apply our criteria to distinguish the characteristics of this structure the following outline emerges:

1. In the hierarchy of groupings, the extended domestic family is not only absolutely predominant but absorbs all other groups.

2. Among the manifestations of sociability, the we-ness predominates over the relations with others; community prevails over the mass and communion which are scarcely apparent; the passive we-ness outweighs the active we-ness.

3. Among the depth levels of social reality which are accented, first come the routine and regular conduct, customary and traditional rather than procedural or ritual. An over-generalization of the situation characteristic of the patriarchal society and structure has led a number of sociologists and philosophers to state that all societies are routinizing, traditional, immobilized and "closed." But this description holds true only for the patriarchal society. Second is the ecological base: the fertility of the extended family, its size, its density, the "natural environment" are part of this base. Rational as well as mystical symbols come third. The social roles come next, that of the eldest son, the benjamin, the adopted and the slave, etc. All the other depth levels remain in the background, including the organizations.

4. The division of technical labor is very slightly developed; the division of social labor is reduced to age and sex groupings and perhaps descendants, slaves and adoptees.

5. In the hierarchy of social regulations or social controls traditional morality and the morality of symbolic ideal images occupy the first position.

6. The cultural works are limited to recited epic traditions, to chants, dances, feasts, to spoken and written language, to cults, rites and religious revelations.

Now we are ready to examine the scale of time corresponding to the patriarchal global structure. Here, the time of slowed down, long duration and retarded time are combined without any difficulty. They are completed by a seasonal as well as religious cyclical time. All of these times lead to a very oppressive stagnation and conservatism in these structures. These conservative social times arise from the predominance of the domestic family and from routine expressed in crystallized patterns customary practices, as well as from the importance of the seasons in the ecological base among other things. Finally, this conservatism also comes from the passive character of the predominating community we-ness and the semi-closed economy in which trade plays an insignificant part.

The scale of social time, characteristic for this structure is:

1. The time of slowed down, long duration.
2. Cyclical time, both mystical and seasonal.
3. Retarded time.
4. Deceptive time.
5. The other times are relegated to the last rung on the scale.

This time scale projects the present into the past glorified by the epic tradition. It turns away from the future and sinks into a boggy quietude much more pronounced than in the so-called archaic structures and in the charismatic-theocratic structures. Nevertheless, the subjacent total social phenomenon despite its very close similarity to the structure, possesses its own movements and scale of time.

1. The time of slowed down, long duration and cyclical time occupy, once more, the first two places. But the increase of population and the scarcities provoked by the increase limit these times of the total social phenomenon to a much greater degree than those of the structure.

2. Retarded time still occupies an important position. Nevertheless, technical patterns are modified at a more accelerated pace.

3. Erratic time, omitted in the time scale of the structure, is in third place in the subjacent total phenomenon. This time is produced by the intra-family conflicts as for example, the intrigues of the benjamin against the eldest brother, the struggles among brothers with different mothers, or between the real sons and the adopted members of the family; finally, there are some movements of discontented slaves. Famines caused by drought, floods, epidemics, or depletion of the soil and invasions and guerilla warfare also produce erratic time.

4. The time alternating between advance and delay arises from innovations in economic activity, from the penetration of trade, and from the application of new technical patterns. This time, more than all the other times, bears witness to the fact that the volcanic forces of the total global social phenomenon are not extinguished in the patriarchal societies. They stay under cover waiting the propitious moment to shake the structure or even to break it. This is a deceptive time where, under the appearance of routine and long duration, there is a veiled thrust to the advance.

Nevertheless, in comparing the time scale of the structure with that of the global social phenomena of the patriarchal society one is struck by the fact that the second only completes the first. Hence, it is this absence of disparity between them which emphasizes the calm routine of this type of society.

This is also expressed in an awareness of time which is extremely limited and does not go much beyond the grasping and symbolizing of the seasons related to agriculture and herding, the life cycle or "ages of man", and the succession of generations. Time is not conceptualized and only very sporadic attempts are made to master it. These are limited to efforts to make the past endure by dissolving the present and future in it. The desire for continuity is so intense that there is an attempt to annihilate not only discontinuity, but all change. This is without success, however.

THE FEUDAL SOCIETIES AND THEIR TIME SCALES

In the feudal societies the situation once again changes radically as do the time scales. Here again the global structure diverges markedly from the subjacent total social phenomenon. The charismatic-theocracy presented, in appearance at least, a unified structure but the feudal type of structure is pluralistic to the extreme. Many hierarchies of groupings and social controls compete and reach a very instable and complex equilibrium. In the charismatic theocracy the time scale of the subjacent, total social phenomenon was visibly more lively, turbulent, more inclined toward advance, and emphasized the future more than did the time scale of the structure. In the feudal type of society we shall observe the exact opposite situation. Here the time scale of the subjacent total social phenomenon favors enduring time and delayed time; the past dominates the present and future in it much more than in the time scale of its structure.

European feudalism is placed between the tenth and fourteenth centuries, generally referred to as the Middle Ages. Historians have noted that feudalism in France, England, Flanders and Germany had certain special traits which made it quite distinct from different forms of feudalism in Russia, Japan, China and so on. One of these traits was the extreme pluralism of multiple but equivalent hierarchies. There were five different, competing hierarchies:

1. *Hierarchized federation of military groupings* based on vassal fealty;

116

the personal commitment of the vassal to the suzerain, and the system oi fiefs wherein the vassal and his domain was protected in return for fulfilment of military obligations.

2. *Hierarchy of patrimonial groupings* whose economic character is manifested in two ways: (1) in the relationship between the manor lord and his serfs and the yeomen of the land with differing rights; (2) in the relationships of the suzerain and his vassals when the fief became hereditary and passed from one generation to the next, affecting both the ownership and the vassal system.

3. *The Hierarchy headed by the monarchic State.* This hierarchy does not appear to be very effective in the Roman-German Empire but rather a loosely organized confederation of suzerains of a given region loosely tied to their feudal king who is only "first among his peers". This State, made up of a block of local groupings, is quite tenuous if not "dormant".

4. *The ecclesiastic Hierarchy of the Roman Church.* This is much different from all the other grouping, federations and hierarchies. The Roman Church is the largest body which plays an important part in feudal society and alone possesses a universal character. The Church's dignitaries were equally a part of the vassal and patrimonial structure, but were subservient only to the ecclesiastic hierarchy. This led first to the bitter quarrels concerning investiture from the eleventh through the thirteenth centuries and then to tendencies to form a theocratic State. In the feudal society the Church is considered above all as the visible incarnation of the *Corpus Mysticum* integrating into its unity the plurality of groupings and their hierarchies. The Church seeks to utilize this position to assert herself as a supra-functional body *par excellence* representing the global social phenomenon. Nevertheless, after numerous conflicts and struggles, the Church is strongly limited by the military preeminence of the feudal bond and by the economic and also the cultural preeminence of the free cities.

5. *The federation of Free Cities and their hierarchies of groupings:* Merchant Guilds, Masters, craftsmen and apprentice associations, etc. The free cities were simultaneously permanent markets, principle centers of industry, trade, finance, international commerce, and banking centers. The city created a special zone in feudal society as is reflected in the common saying, "City air makes one free". The eminent Belgian historian Henri Pirenne, speaks of the "veritable municipal revolution" in that the free cities established their own provisionary governments. This much is

certain: The free cities acquired an independence and sufficient power to compete seriously with the feudal and patrimonial hierarchy as well as with the Church and the State. The atmosphere of the city is that of accumulated wealth, struggles between merchant guilds and artisans, the masters, craftsmen and apprentices. It is an atmosphere of rationalism, intellectual activity and the classical tradition. The rational influence of the city penetrated into the universities which were located there although they were ecclesiastic establishments. In this manner Thomism replaced Augustinianism.

To summarize the general characteristics of the global structure of feudal society:

(a) In the competition between the feudal bond, patrimonial bond, the Church, the federation of free cities and finally the dormant or almost dormant State, the Church tends toward a certain preeminence but is limited by the growing importance of the free cities. There is a considerable profusion of special groupings, often non-territorial.

(b) There is a preponderance of the we-nesses over the relations with others, but the interindividual and intergroup relations with others develop more than expected.

Among the we-nesses, community exerts a strong influence. Sometimes it is active as in the cities, in the different merchant and craft corporations, brotherhoods, associations, orders of knighthood, religious orders, etc. Sometimes it is passive as in the manors, among the patrimonial groups, in the villages, in the conjugal families. These community we-nesses are limited by communions and passive masses in the Church and State.

(c) The levels of social reality accentuated are the social roles variously interpreted, collective attitudes, mystic and rational symbols, ideas and values and collective mentality. The level of organization and the ecological base compete.

(d) If the technical division of labor is somewhat rudimentary, except among the artisans in the cities, the divisions of social labor, in contrast, is very pronounced.

(e) In social control law, religion and art are more important than education and morality. These three also predominate over knowledge. Philosophical and theological knowledge occupy first place in the latter domain.

(f) In the system of cultural works although Christianity has priority,

118

the Hellenic tradition, Roman culture, barbarian-germanic and Moorish influences have penetrated feudal society. Yet the idea of *Corpus Mysticum* and of *aevum* intermediate between *aeternitas* and *tempus*, dominates this global society. To be sure, this central orientation is limited by the increasing rational and utilitarian spirit of the cities.

It is difficult to establish a time scale for this structure since there are five competing hierarchies. Only in the patrimonial structure the time of slowed down, long duration predominates. The hierarchy of vassalage, with its contractual form of investiture and fealty, requires a vast organization. Within it deceptive time predominates and a time alternating between advance and delay is hidden under the slowed down, retarded time. Deceptive time also applies to the Church because of its vast and powerful organization. Therefore, cyclical time of the religious rites is limited here both by deceptive time and time alternating between advance and delay which arises from the secular activities of the Church, its involvement in political, juridical, and economic struggles as much as this alternating irregular time manifests itself in theological discussions, heresies, ecstatic experiences and religious laxity. The Church plays an important role in conceptualizing, as well as in measuring times with the influence of Christian rites and festivals, as well as of Greek and Latin traditions. Thus the time scale of the Church in feudal society is in itself very complex.

Finally, if the dormant State lives in a time lagging behind the federation of free cities lives in a time pushing forward, approaching explosive time. The time alternating between advance and delay, erratic time, deceptive time and time behind itself do limit this explosive, creative time by projecting the present into the future. The time of the Church and the time of the free cities have a tendency to predominate in the time scale of the global feudal structure where the time of the vassal bond is relegated to the third position. With this in mind, the following is an approximate outline of feudal structure time scale.

1. Deceptive time, concealing many surprises.

2. The time alternating between advance and delay arising from the accentuation of social roles, the conflict between the different, equivalent hierarchies; and finally from the manifestations of active community wenesses.

3. The time of sharp struggle between the time of advance and delay

intervenes when an alternation between the two times cannot be attained.

4. The time leaping forward in the cities, the time behind itself and the time of long duration in the country.

5. Erratic time, due as much to the perpetual struggles and conflicts between hierarchies of groups belonging to this structure as to the unexpected mobility of the demographical aspect.

6. Cyclical time, both seasonal and mystical, plays a far less important role than one would expect.

To summarize, the social time scale of the feudal structures favors more than one would think, the time alternating between advance and delay, the time ahead of itself and erratic time. This has repercussions for the theological doctrines of the Middle Ages which have distinguished, as is mentioned above, between *aeternitas*, *aevum* and *tempus* – divine time, intermediary time and human time. These doctrines attribute to the Church – the visible *Corpus Mysticum* – the capacity to live intermediary time (*aevum*), permit society and man, under Church direction to surpass themselves by precipitating an advance towards the future. Evidently, this is a compromise. But this compromise witnesses to the fact that the time pushing forward was very much present in the feudal structure as the crusades illustrate. This intermediary time haunted the conscience of the medieval man. It is necessary to add that *aevum* had also a totally different aspect when it was a matter of individual fanatics or masses terrorized by the fear of heresy and hell. This time often appeared to them as the time of the end of the world, the time of the apocalypse, which seemed to them at certain moments to be so near.

It is perhaps here that the tension between the time scale of the feudal structure and that of its subjacent total social phenomenon becomes particularly clear. Actually the time scale of the total social phenomenon of feudal society was very much behind that of its structure.

In this second time scale, that of the subjacent total phenomenon, first place is occupied once again by the time of long duration and slow motion. Second is cyclical time which is half mystical and half seasonal. The third place is left to the time behind itself. These same three times are the most important in the patriarchal society. In the feudal society which concerns us here, these three times of the subjacent total phenomenon were reinforced by a mystical faith and symbolism which depended on fear and fanaticism. The heavy burden of the total social phenomenon's time scale has cut or at least slowed down the push of the corresponding structure's time scale. The divergency, competition and interpenetration of these two time scales has, therefore, tended to complicate the already tormented life of the feudal societies.

As to the awareness of time and time scales, or in other words, the act of seizing hold of them, perceiving, symbolizing, conceptualizing and measuring these times, the Church has been the most active. Thus, the Gregorian calendar, as opposed to the Julian was under its control and linked closely with the celebration of the Saints' days and other religious festivals. The schedule of the peasant life depended on the sounding of the parish church bells. Moreover, at the beginning of the thirteenth century, and above all the fourteenth century, these bells were adjusted to sound more often. It is interesting to note that this resulted in the appearance of clocks. This invention was probably due as well to the development of technical skill as to the combined influence of the free cities and the more intensive revival of the Greco-Latin tradition.

The free cities which sheltered the universities, which in turn depended on the Church, played a separate role in the becoming aware and measuring of time. Here, awareness of time, being much different from that of the Church, did influence the latter. The markets, commercial and maritime communications, corporation and municipal elections all furnished a new outlook and new points of reference for the perception, conceptualization and measuring of time and thus manifested human time (*tempus*). These points of reference were evidently quite different from those of religious festivals and ritual, and more largely from *aevum*.

Only the Church tried to master time. The distinction between *aeternitas, aevum* and *tempus* is one aspect of this. The manipulation and the control of the calendar is another. The fear of an impending apocalypse is also a repercussion of this desire to master time. The only competition comes once again from the federation of the free cities. The inclination to master time is manifested by the interest shown in the ancient classical and philosophical theories and through the tendency to quantify time. The cities thus became centers in which the Renaissance found its support. It is true that neither the Church nor the free cities succeeded in mastering the time scales corresponding to the structure and the total social phenomenon of feudal society. If they had succeeded, feudal society would have been transformed into either a world theocracy or a confederation of free

121

urban republics. It is the unforeseen alliance between the territorial State and the newly born town-bourgeoisie which provoked the establishment of a new society with its own time scale. This new type is the first phase of capitalism combined with absolute monarchy.

However, before we move to a consideration of nascent capitalism we must look at the classical City-States becoming Empires.

THE ANCIENT CITY-STATES BECOMING EMPIRES AND THEIR TIME SCALES

In contrast to the theocratic-charismatic and feudal types of society, here we find a relatively reduced divergency between the global structure and the total social phenomenon. There is no dramatic contradiction between the two scales of time. On the contrary they combine. But in contrast to the theocratic-charismatic and patriarchal societies, the scale of the total subjacent phenomenon lags behind the time scale of this society's structure. The time scale of this structure is thereby limited in its push forward.

The type of global society where the City-State on the way to becoming an Empire predominates is well known. The Greek *polis* of the seventh through the fifth centuries B.C. and the Latin *civitas* offer us classic examples of this type of global society. Certain analogous characteristics are discovered in the Italian cities of the Renaissance in spite of the differences in their historical destiny.

In this type of society, a specific territorial group is pre-eminent. The city or town symbolizes the principle of locality and neighborhood. These locality groups predominate over kinship groupings of gens, gentes, curia, phratries and over those of religious belief. Here the Church is only a subordinate organ of the City-State. The City-State also dominates the extended families to which the slaves are attached. It predominates over the artisan associations, brotherhoods, sodalities and collegia, over the economic strata and so on.

The city domination over all the other groupings is accompanied by a tendency to favor the secular and the rational and by the differentiation of law, morals, as well as philosophical, scientific and political knowledge. The City-State develops scientific and political knowledge while religion and magic are forced into the background. The Natural is victorious over the supernatural. The global social structure is democratized at the same

122

rate as the reinforcement of the territorial principle and the emphasis on the superiority of human reason. Individualism triumphed in Rome through the intermediary of Roman law, favoring at the same time the *dominum* and the *imperium*. This individualism dominated in Greece not only in the democratic political organs and judicial procedures, but also in art, philosophy, in the doctrines of the Sophists of Socrates, of the Stoics, the Epicureans, the Sceptics, and the Cynics. It had equal importance in art, mores, and customs, in exchanges of all kinds, even in the principle of dialogue and in the Greek tragedies where man struggled against his destiny.

Technical knowledge and economic life were both very much behind development in philosophy and scientific knowledge, art, law and political organization. Neither the Greeks nor the Romans harnessed the horse for agriculture. They were only used in ceremonies of State display and in combat. Agriculture and animal husbandry remained at a very undeveloped level. The technical division of labor was far behind the social division of labor. This is explained by the importance of slavery and the negative attitude toward agricultural and industrial work. Other than the looting of the conquered towns, the principal sources for accumulation of great wealth lay in large scale trade and especially maritime commerce in which the Greeks excelled, military conquest at which the Romans were strongest, and finally, financial speculation and the land grabbing activities of the proconsuls in the distant provinces of the Empire.

The pronounced economic inequalities, the movements of great masses of admitted aliens *(métèques)* and ruined citizens of defunct City-States of Greece, the hungry people asking for *"panem et circenses"*, and finally the revolt of slaves, all of these phenomena might create the impression that there were at least embryonic social classes. This was true, above all, at the moment when the decomposition of these social structures was manifested in the Greek Tyrannies and in the Roman Praetorian regime. Nevertheless, the mentioned phenomena cannot be called social classes. For one thing, the suffering groups were not at all impervious to the global society. Next, they possessed neither class consciousness nor class ideology, nor was there any specific structuration. Add to this the fact that, except for the slaves, they played very seldom a role in production and that it was impossible for them to communicate with the strata of the same level in other City-State-Empires.

We can now characterize the structure of this type of society according to our usual criteria:

(a) The city-metropolis predominates over all the other functional groupings such as the extended domestic families including the slaves, the groupings of origin and of birth such as the eupatrides, demos, patricians and plebians, census groupings, military groupings, groupings of economic activity and affinity and finally the mystic-ecstatic groupings of priests, the augurs of Roman antiquity, those grouped around mysteries and oracles in Greece. These latter groupings played a subordinate role in the secular City-States. Among these groupings only the extended families and hereditary groupings, as far as they existed, effectively limited the all-pervasive power of the City-State. All the others were very weak in their relation to the City-State which dominated them just as it reduced the whole of the people to a dust of individuals whether they were citizens or aliens.

(b) The we-nesses were strongly limited by relations with others. These interindividual and intergroup relations predominate over all partial fusions. The broad accentuation of individualism which was manifested in all domains and in all forms was derived from this. This individualism does not contradict the domination of the State which vascillated in the dust of dispersed individuals. The We-nesses asserted itself most strongly in the city, where active and rational community was both the source and the pillar of the flourishing ancient cities. They united very easily in the development of relations with others. They contributed to the development of organizations, jural and secular social control and political democracy.

(c) First among the depth levels here are the patterns, rules and signs which are rational and unencumbered by routine or tradition. They are on the contrary innovating and changing and promote the new. They are consciously linked to human will and reason which invented and created them and they continue to serve as points of reference for social transformation. These depth levels are linked with the confidence in human creative power and the future of society. Thus we have the famous reforms of *Solon, Clisthenes* and *Pericles* in Greece; the success of the reforms of the Law of the *Twelve Tables*, those of *Servius Tullius* and of the *Lex Hortensia* of Rome.

Organization is in second place. It is guided by rules and only becomes

124

encumbering and crumbles under the Roman Empire. Often rational ideas and values, usually linked to philosophical and scientific knowledge, art and law, as well as collective mentality, shows confidence in new experiences, original judgments and intuitions.

The ecological and demographic base remains very important. Innovating social roles such as tribune, orator, demagogue, conspirator, wise men philosopher, sophist, statesman, reformer, military leader, praetorian, free man, rich man of commerce, etc., emphasize the creative and are accentuated much more than the social roles that encourage the routinized conduct of procedural rites, customs and mores. The former roles are examples of conscious innovation and favor time leaping forward and erratic time.

(d) The technical division of labor is, as we have already remarked, much more retarded than we would have expected here if we were to refer to the general scope and richness of this civilization, its development in commerce, and accumulation of wealth, its political and military strength. The social division of labor is much more advanced even among the teams of slaves. The accumulation of wealth is facilitated by the intensive development of money circulation. The existence of different denominations of coins makes it possible for all strata to have access to this money.

(e) Knowledge, law, and art compete in the hierarchy of social control. These three are followed by morality and education. Religion and mythology occupy the last rung.

What, then, is the time scale of the ancient City-State becoming Empire? Within the atmosphere of these structures time leaping forward and explosive time of creation, differentiated from all other social times, entered, without camouflage in the semi-official time scale. "The Greek miracle" and more generally, "the miracle of ancient, rational humanism" has been precisely the possibility for this structure to move in a time pushing forward where the future is rendered present. In the social patterns and regulations of this structure, in the action of the City-State-Empire the future is emphasized. In political and social struggles as well as in the reforms of Athenian structures and the initiatives of republican and imperial Rome, in the great colonial enterprises, both maritime or military, the time leaping forward plays a decisive role. The present is projected into the future and the future in the present; in other words, future and present interpenetrate as they both turn away from the past. This accession of the time pushing forward in the time scale of the global structure was limited only to the reality of fact.

There was *a consciousness of this accession* which was seen as a freeing of human life and was a source of creativity. It was conceptualized in Greek philosophy and sciences as well as in their artistic and literary works. There was an effort to master the time scale by putting time pushing forward in first place. This was the effort of the leaders of the city-state-empire and political men. What we want to underline is that if we distinguish between the real time scale, the awareness of time, and the effort to master it, time pushing forward is much more accentuated in the consciousness, in the thought, in the whole struggle to master time than in the real time scale. We shall return to this awareness and mastery of time in the City-States. First however, let us concentrate on the real time scale.

Despite its clear-cut appearence, the time leaping forward does not succeed in achieving first place in the hierarchy of times. It is, in fact, strongly checked by the time lagging behind which is characteristic of the domestic family groupings since they are very much weighed down by slavery, which predominates in the rural areas. It must not be forgotten that the large Town-Cities and all their activity are the exception and that the rural areas are predominant. The time of delay in the rural areas is reinforced not only by routine and traditional patterns but by the religious and mythological beliefs in which those patterns find refuge. These evolve and favor cyclical time, bogged down even more by the intervention of the time of long duration and slow motion. The ecological base, which retains its great importance in the structure, along with the disproportionately rudimentary technical skills, finds its cadence in this time of long duration and slow motion. In addition, the springboard for time pushing forward is found in these structures, first in the rules and secondly in the organization. When the two are crystallized they tend to favor time lagging behind or at least deceptive time. Hence time pushing forward is restrained from the start. This load which it would have to carry is much too heavy. This observation is reinforced by the fact that the total social phenomena, subjacent to these structures move in a time torn by the irreconcilable conflict between the time of the cities and the time of the rural areas.

Thus, the actual time scale of the global structure of this type of society is not exactly as would be expected.

1. In the first place is the persistent struggle between the time pushing forward and time lagging behind.

2. In second place is the erratic time of the agitated activity of the cities with their ebb and flow of increasingly varied populations and internal conflicts struggling with the time of long duration and slow motion belonging to the rural areas. Erratic time can be allied not only with the time pushing forward but also with other times such as the alternating time and the time of persistent struggle between advance and delay.

3. The third rung contains deceptive time aligned with the organizations, which in turn favor time of delay as well as the time of advance. But, under the rule of the tyrants and the Caesars, the organizations had to submit to frequent crises and thereby found themselves confronted by a totally disorganized society. Thus here, deceptive time was often allied with erratic time.

4. The explosive time of creation only appears at special moments of important reforms and in the works of art, science and philosophy.

5. Finally, cyclical time, mythological or natural, and more often both at the same time, is only manifested in rural life.

The total social phenomenon of this type of global society evolves in a time scale which favors time pushing forward still less than is the case for the structure.

1. Here the time lagging behind competes with the time alternating between advance and delay and takes over the first place.

2. Time of long duration and slow motion follows next.

3. Deceptive time comes then. It favors delay (slavery) under the appearance of advance.

4. Erratic time occupies the fourth rung. It is introduced by wars, invasions and famines.

5. The time pushing forward is thus forced to fifth place and finds serious competition in cyclical time.

In this type of society, the awareness of time is usually the work of philosophers, artists and scientists. Plotinus intended to suppress time, dissolving cyclical time in the "living eternity". Plato, while affirming eternity symbolized by the immobility of ideas, admitted nevertheless, that time under the form of Eros is pushing the tangible world towards these same ideas. Heraclites, Pythagoras, the Sophists, and Aristotle tried by different approaches to conceptualize time. Pythagoras and Aristotle

127

attempted to measure it and to quantify it by submitting the movement of time to numbers. The results were meagre.

As to the mastery of time, the heads of State and the political men attempted to dominate time. They had partially succeeded in accomplishing this over many long centuries. But their relative success was not sufficient to free this structure and this society from the heavy burden of delay which arrested their push.

This enormous slowing down due to a slave economy, poor technique and a State oscillating in the vacuum created by the absence of free and strong groupings, was the principle cause of the incapacity of the society of this type to resist the invasion of the barbarians to which it succumbed.

CHAPTER VIII

THE TIME SCALES OF MODERN SOCIETIES

NASCENT CAPITALISTIC GLOBAL SOCIETIES
AND THEIR TIME SCALES

We move now to the study of the social time scale of the type of society which gave birth to nascent capitalism and "enlightened" absolutism. This type of global society has been described and analyzed many times by economists, historians and sociologists. The first volume of *Das Kapital* by Karl Marx contains excellent material on the first phases of the accumulation of capital. The development of technology, industrialization and mechanization, the clear awareness of practical power which the man of knowledge acquired, particularly the man of *technological knowledge* allowed him to control nature and other men. Finally, the first symptoms of the dissolution of all the forces mediating between the individual and the State to the advantage of *laissez faire* capitalism were the most important traits of this society. Incipient mechanization, industrialization, the appearance of real social classes, a substantial reduction of the divergency between the structure and the subjacent total social phenomenon fundamentally distinguish the society of this type from the ancient City-State, despite certain historical similarities underlined by the Renaissance. In the beginning the development of technology and industrialization did not exclude anxieties nor strong religious reactions but the development of the society of this type is linked with the rationalism pushing toward the enlightenment-period. In Western Europe, this phase of capitalism covered the seventeenth and eighteenth centuries, although it was already initiated in the second half of the sixteenth century.

In the structures of this global society, the vast territorial, monarchic State, allied itself with the bourgeoisie of the cities and with the civil servant nobility. This alliance predominated over the church, the military nobility, the clergy and the third estate, the peasants, the religious and political factions as well as over the economic enterprises, which the State had itself stimulated and sometimes founded. Such were the chartered manufacturers who also competed with the old corporations of crafts and guilds. The State also dominated the workers assembled in the mills and factories. This working population was recruited from among the most impoverished elements of the cities and the rural areas where the exactions of the lords and the concomitant misery compelled some of the peasants to abandon their fields and become workers.

In the global society of this type for the first time, as we have already mentioned, the differentiation into social classes appears. The social class is manifested outside the official frameworks and competes with the hierarchy of functional groupings and their entrenched "Order". The territorial monarchial State supported the bourgeois Commoners, the industrial capitalists, merchants and bankers from whom the king borrowed money. Their wealth was considerably increased after the discovery of the New World. They were promoted against the nobility, or at least the military nobility, and against the workers and the peasants; these promotion accelerated the overthrow of the former hierarchy. In the beginning, the State kept the social classes well in hand, at least as well as it kept the "official orders". It watched over industrialization, particularly in metallurgy and textiles, and supported capitalism, to reinforce its own economic military and financial situation. But soon the State came to play the role of the "Sorcerer-Apprentice" and instead of dominating the social classes, it was dominated by them.

The continued improvement of technological and economic patterns grew in importance. Nevertheless, new invention and their application came at irregular and slowed down intervals because the economic organization including the residues of craft-corporations and guilds, and the demographic movement lagged behind technology. Elsewhere, the total social phenomenon, slowed by the non-productive "Estates" and by stagnation in the rural areas which only budged under the influence of the cities and the State, limited the creative thrust of technical and industrial development.

Compensating for this, philosophy, influenced by the sciences, was oriented towards a new humanistic and promethean rationalism. This rationalism, was linked with an idealism and an individualism appealing to the conscience of the *self* as the unique and exclusive center of Reason. It inspired in man an inextinguishable confidence in the success of his enterprises, including his technological and industrial endeavors. Accord-

130

ing to the viewpoint of this philosophy and attitude, man has no time to loose. Thus, time is most precious; it is the producer of wealth and power. "Time is money". Even more, laziness, delay and wasted time are the sources of all evil. These affirmations were already found in Bacon, Macchiavelli, and Erasmus. Also subscribing to it very willingly were Descartes, Locke, Leibniz, and of course the Encyclopedists. The famous *Encyclopedia* carries as its sub-title, *Rational Dictionary of Arts and Crafts*. But, the arts and crafts are tied to the effort to gain time, and the tendency to quantify social time so accentuated in this structure, is considered as a means of eliminating the *loss of time*, or in any case, of limiting this loss.

Let us outline the traits of the global structure of the society of this type according to our usual criteria:

(a) The territorial monarchy predominates at every point over the other groupings even though they possess much more power and effectiveness than in the ancient City-State. The official hierarchy of the constituting orders were the nobility, clergy, the Third Estate, and the peasants. Included among the latter were farmers of different kinds: few property owners, a majority of tenants, some salaried people; most of them paid manorial rights, tithes and tolls. There were various ranks of the nobility, such as civil servants whose offices were purchased, and the military nobility of more or less hereditary character. Other levels included the residue of artisan corporations craft-unions and guilds. This whole official hierarchy was threatened internally by the incipient social classes which were struggling to dominate the State. New economic enterprises of great scope such as factories, mills, societies of maritime commerce, etc., at first favored by the monarchy finally became hostile to it. They did not approve of the politics of war nor of maintaining the privileges of the nobility.

(b) Among the we-nesses, the passive masses predominate in the society. The partial fusions are strongly limited by considerable development of active relations with Others. The politics of leveling, so dear to the absolute monarchy, combined with the rise of manufacturing, the movement of the wealthy to large cities, the disintegration of the feudal manorial regimes in the rural areas, created conditions to enhance the accentuation of Masses. These masses predominated in the State, in urban life, partially in rural life, in capitalistic enterprises, in the reorganized armies and lastly in the emerging social classes, particularly in the working class. The community we-nesses were found only in disintegrating craft-corporations and also in the rising bourgeois class. A very developed relation with Others, limiting the we-nesses was favored in all kinds of exchanges and contracts. The full range of these interpersonal and intergroup relations was nevertheless impeded by vestiges of the privileged estates and of the barriers thrown up between them along with interference in the economic life by the enlightened absolute monarchy.

(c) The predominating depth level is that of patterns relating equally to juridical rule and technological models. These two kinds of patterns are innovating. The minute and penetrating jural regulations, coming from above, combat the outmoded customs and practices. The new technological patterns revolutionize economic life. These two kinds of patterns are often combined, but can also compete and be in conflict. The ecological demographic base comes next. Its importance is derived from the need for manual labor and the problem of its recruitment. The third rung is occupied by organizations and by social roles. Finally, symbols, rational and innovating ideas and values encourage the members of this society to take the initiative to dominate both nature and society. However, they are not always successful.

(d) The enormous pressure for the technical division of labor combined with mechanization, leads to an incomparable productivity growing both in quantity and quality. The social division of labor is far outdistanced by technological division of labor. The accumulation of wealth increases without precedence and is augmented by the discovery of the New World. The accumulation of wealth is accompanied by great contrasts between poverty and wealth.

(e) In the hierarchy of social control, knowledge and law compete for first place; scientific and technical compete with philosophical knowledge; law is mostly legislative or by royal ordinance. Education is in second place as it begins to be freed from ecclesiastic tutelage; morality, art and religion come next.

(f) As to the cultural aspect, the natural is victorious over the supernatural, individualism increases in all domains and the idea of the "progress of consciousness" is born.

We can now deal with the social time scale corresponding to the global social structure of this type and to its subjacent total social phenomenon.

132

(1) Time alternating between advance and delay is first. This alternating time is characteristic of the succession of technological inventions which play an important role. Nevertheless, their applications are interrupted by more or less long intervals and meet with unexpected difficulties. This same alternating time is manifested in the political and juridical life of the monarchies, in the cadence of the relations among the three Estates, between the cities and the country, between the nobility and the bourgeoisie, not to mention the fact that this time favors the rising bourgeoisie. Alternating time intervenes in the development of manufacturing plants, factories, and mills, commerce, in fact in all of economic life. This alternating time is also characteristic of the demographic make-up of cities, the religious struggles, and the relations between State and Church. Finally, this time characterizes the very existence of this whole global structure which is simultaneously anachronistic and innovating.

(2) Erratic time occupies second place in this time scale. It is characteristic of the new working class; not yet class conscious, crippled by the new situation in which it finds itself, intimidated by the machines which could menace its earning power. In sum, this class is in total upheaval. The accentuation of mass situations and their diffusion in vast collectivities favor irregular pulsations, reinforced again by fearful economic inequalities, by the disintegration of the craft corporations and fraternities, by the ebb and flow of international relations, and by the contrasts between the Old and New World. The already uncertain time alternating between advance and delay receives here a special accent on insecurity and harassment from erratic time. There is, therefore, no way for alternating time to move from the present and from the past toward the future.

(3) In third place in this scale of time is time leaping forward manifested in the growing cities, in the manufacturing plants and also in the State. The time lagging behind is dominant in the rural areas, in the Church, and in the nobility.

(4) The time of persistent struggle between advance and delay is manifested particularly in the conflict which takes place in the collective mentality between the cultural works, symbols, values and ideas of the bourgeois ideology and that of the Estates and privileged groups. The latter more than the representatives of the former furnish Royalty with its intimate entourage save for some exceptional, well known men such as Colbert, Turgot or Necker.

(5) The time of slowed down, long duration belongs particularly to the ecological base because of the demographic problems of this society and also the constant efforts to discover and accumulate raw materials.

(6) Deceptive time and cyclical time are not important in the time scale of these structures, for organizations are only strong in the political domain where they are influenced by initatives "from above". In the economic domain, former corporations are rapidly disintegrating even though the new industrial organizations and especially those of professions are only latent.

We can now contrast the global structure time scale with that of the total social phenomenon. Paradoxically, the time of the total social phenomenon is partly behind and partly ahead of its own structure. In industrial technology, international commerce and scientific knowledge, both technical and philosophical, the bourgeois class and its ideology, are essentially in advance. The nobility and the clergy, the agrarian economy, the restrictions placed on economic organization, and the peasantry are in retardation. The absolute monarchy itself advances by taking important initiatives but it is retarded in its organization. This second time scale could be expressed as follows:

(1) In first place is the time of persistent struggle between advance and delay, a struggle wherein time leaping forward makes some progress.

(2) Deceptive time is second. It characterizes the superimposed organizations as much as it does the ambivalent atmosphere of the total social phenomenon. This atmosphere is full of internal contradictions and under the appearance of a compromise hides the virtuality of sudden crises.

(3) The time lagging behind is third. All resistance and obstacles to peaceful reform of this structure move within this time.

(4) Fourth are alternating time, erratic time and the time of long duration in never-ending competition and conflict.

The time scale of the subjacent total social phenomenon is much more harassed than that of the structure in this type of society.

Thus, the rumble of explosive time of creation, collective and individual, makes itself felt and is directly manifested in the English and Dutch revolutions, in the civil and religious wars, and the war of independence of the United States. But it is particularly during the great French Revolution that this time takes on exceptional prominence, never again to be forgotten by the collective memory. The spectacular explosion of the "Old

Regime" global structure, therefore, made its indelible imprint on the new social structures which emerged from the Revolution.

In the society of this type, the awareness of time and of the time scale, the grasping, perceiving and conceptualizing of time usually is taken over by the State, on the one hand, and by the bourgeoisie on the other hand. Both the State and the bourgeoisie are linked with science and technology which push for the quantification of time. The State intervenes to reorganize teaching and assists it to become rationalized and modernized. It founds new schools, technical and professional, such as school of mines, bridges, and causeways, sea, artillery, etc. It creates those of secondary or advanced education such as the College of France, the Academies, etc. From the pressure of these establishments, as well as the teaching of recent scientific and technical discoveries, the conceptualization of this quantified time is expanded. The bourgeoisie in its turn is aware of time in its quantified form and applies it to its economic enterprises ("time is money" becomes official), displays it clothed in the ideology of "automatic progress" which would follow inexorably from the simple accumulation of efforts by the succeeding generations. The newly formed classes of workers and *petit* bourgeois are not directly aware of their time. The established bodies such as the nobility and clergy resist the new time of the Age of Enlightenment, refusing to accept the modified scale of time, and are aware only of their own time which lags very much behind.

As to the mastery of the time, the monarchic State utilizes enlightened absolutism to maintain a balance between time of advance and time of delay. It does this in order to dominate the erratic time of Masses, which it has itself promoted by favoring industrialization, and the erratic time of social classes competing with the official, already disintegrating, social hierarchy. This mastery of time succeeded in western societies up to the French Revolution and was maintained up to the end of the nineteenth century in Central and Eastern Europe, as for example in Germany, Austria, Hungary, and Czarist Russia.

THE TIME SCALES OF THE DEMOCRATIC-LIBERAL GLOBAL SOCIETIES WITH DEVELOPED COMPETITIVE CAPITALISM

The global society of this type dominated Europe and America in the

nineteenth century and at the beginning of the twentieth century. Following the British, American and above all the French revolutions, this
society developed parliamentary regimes and customs and grew in the
majority of the Western countries, particularly in England, Holland, in
the Scandinavian countries and finally in France. This regime is characterized by the triumph of the principles enunciated in the *Declaration of
the Rights of Man and of the Citizen* (1789). These were combined with
universal suffrage, and legislative power predominated over executive
power, most often through a parliament. In other words, government was
responsible to and dependent on a parliamentary majority, on the freedom and influence of a plurality of political parties, labor unions and
employer associations and so on. Freedom was granted to industrial
concerns, trusts and cartels, State and Church were separated. The democratic and secular territorial State remained at the summit of all functional
groupings. Under certain conditions, it enlarged its sphere of influence:
(a) by interfering in the economic life of the economic society and its
struggles; (b) by colonial politics which opened up new markets; (c) by its
agrarian policy and custom control; (d) by its often desperate efforts to
combat unemployment and economic crises; (e) by its social legislation
protecting the weak and those who were economically dispossessed; (f) by
seeking to create the general frameworks within which to facilitate
collective labor agreements; (g) in the cultural life, by the organization of
public education at every level.

Nevertheless, its ability to dominate the economic life and directly
influence its powerful organizations was often less than that of the "old
order". There were several reasons for this. First of all, the democratic
territorial State was dominated by the industrial, financial, commercial
bourgeoisie, sometimes alone, sometimes in liaison with the middle classes
and with the rich farmers. Their particular economic interests pressed
heavily on the State. Second, private disciplinary and regulatory power
was always exercised internally by the management or owners of these
great factories and enterprises to which millions of workers submitted in
their daily life. The development of this arbitrary power limited the
authority of the State and threatened to transform itself into a kind of
"economic feudalism".

The technological or economic patterns as well as the organization of
the industrial plants, become decisive in this global social structure. The

complete mechanization, the assembly line, huge industry, oil and gasoline, electrification, the unbelievable acceleration of transportation through railroad, steamboat and automobile and of communication through telegraph and telephone, cause technological equipment to be the very base of society's existence and its prosperity. The nations competed from the standpoint of the extent of their industrialization. Also within each society the competition between the Capitalist enterprises reach its zenith in terms of their modernization. The investment of capital in machinery leads finally to a considerable reduction of profits. In spite of economic crises on a world-wide scale, in spite of periodic unemployment, in spite of the class struggles which become more and more acute, in spite of the development of the labor movement and its organization in political parties and trade unions, in of spite International Socialist Organizations and events such as the Commune of Paris; finally, in spite of the menace of imperialist and colonial wars, this is the greatest epoch of capitalism. Competitive capitalism seems to favor the expansion of production, the acceleration of technical inventions, the promotion of heightened level of consumption even among the proletariat. This orientation is so marked that capitalism is assured of not only the colonial markets but also the markets of technologically underdeveloped countries.

To summarize our description of the characteristics of this global structure:

(a) The liberal-democratic, territorial State remains at the head of the functional groupings. Nevertheless, collectivities such as industrial and financial enterprises, trusts and cartels, employer associations and labor unions have a tendency to compete with the State and to threaten its authority. As the social classes struggle among themselves and with the State they augment the instability of this hierarchy even though they constitute its foundation, except when one class finally succeeds in dominating. The different techno-bureaucratic groupings of foremen, general managers, commercial financial managers of business concerns, engineers, experts, high-placed plublic servants, military officers of the upper ranks, etc... become exceedingly important. Marx[1], in his day, was

---

[1] See the quotations from *Das Kapital* on this subject, as presented in my public lectures at the Sorbonne published under the title *Le concept de classes sociales de Marx à nos jours*, Paris, 1954; 2nd ed., 1960, pp. 37–39 and in *La vocation actuelle de la sociologie*, V, Vol. II, 2nd ed., 1963, pp. 313–317.

already aware of their existence and influence. These groupings are distributed diversely among the varied classes.

(b) There is a general tendency to favor the predominance of active masses, now scattered, now assembled. Active community we-nesses are found pre-eminently in the bourgeois class: for example, employer organizations. Active communions tend to be accented in the proletarian class, in labor unions and in political parties representing labor. Elsewhere, the we-nesses are strongly limited by relations with Others, especially observable in active intergroup and interindividual relations. The competitive orientation of this social structure reaches full height here.

(c) It is obvious that technical and economic patterns are more accentuated here than all the others levels of social reality. Those who affirm the "pre-eminence of technology in social life" (for example, L. Mumford in *Technics and Civilization*, 1939, and before him W. F. Ogburn, *Social Change*, 1923, 11th ed., 1950, along with the great American economist Veblen who was their predecessor), are perfectly correct in their assessment, but *only for the global social structure of this type* and not for any other. The social classes, labor unions, and political parties which represent them hold so important a place in this social structure that their social roles, collective attitudes, as well as the roles of their leaders, of their militant supporters, of their adversaries, must be put in second place immediately after the technical and economic patterns. These roles can be collective as well as individual, and carry an element of surprise which can lead to desired roles acquired after some very difficult struggles. The Organization-level holds the third place for instance in the economic life (the administration of the large business concerns, trusts and cartels), as well as in the social and political struggles (union federations, their central offices, the general staff of political parties). To this is added the growth of the administrative staff of the State and of its public services, for instance those which strengthen transportation and communication. The ecological base continues to be accentuated but its importance decreases.

(d) Technical division of labor and the social division of labor are fully developed. The complete mechanization only provokes a redistribution of these divisions and a new balance among them, but not their diminution.

(e) At the head of the system of social control is found scientific knowledge, followed closely by technical knowledge as well as "political knowledge" or "ideology" in the strict sense of the term. Next is secular education and instruction, then jural regulations transcending legislation and resting upon autonomous groupings and collective labor agreements. Finally, we find morality, particularly morality of aspiration and of symbolic ideal images, belonging to the proletarian class and even to the bourgeois class, so far as the last is not entirely given to utilitarian or imperative morality.

(f) Science and the cult of scientific knowledge (scientism), which is expected to solve every problem, play a role of first importance in the cultural works characteristic of this structure.

These are the basic characteristics of the democratic-liberal type of structure. Now we shall look at the time scale corresponding to this structure. Then we shall want to know if the structure and the subjacent total social phenomenon are divergent in this type of society.

Although the bourgeoisie is the dominant class in this structure, and in spite of its tendency to conceptualize time as quasi-universal and quantitative, it does not succeed in imposing its time scale on the global structure of this society. In a previous chapter we brought out the fact the bourgeoisie, because it always has a considerable economic position to defend and property to protect, lives in a much more conservative time scale than would be expected. The first two places in this time scale are occupied by time alternating between advance and delay and deceptive time where delay is masked and appears as advance.

The depth level of technological and economic patterns is strongly accented in this structure. These patterns favor time alternating between advance and delay and we might therefore expect that this would be the predominant time in the liberal democratic structure. Nevertheless, the situation is much more complex. The bourgeoisie can oppose new technical inventions as strongly as it favors their adoption.

The force of the class struggles, the unexpected economic crises which become increasingly acute, the growth of unionism, the important conflicts between political parties, the precipitation of the rural population's exodus to the cities, the extraordinary development of the big cities, the seizure by competitive capitalist countries of foreign lands for purposes of establishing markets and colonies, the growing fatigue of all acquired symbols and the growing uncertainty in the economic, political, intellectual sphere – all these tendencies seem to push these structures to give top priority to time pushing forward.

139

This time pushing forward, which struggled vainly for first place in the structure of the ancient City-States, and in enlightened monarchy, at least partly succeeds in the liberal democratic structure. But it is challenged by the time alternating between advance and delay derived from the resistance of the privileged groups within the bourgeoisie, and from their going backwards when menaced by overproduction and the reduction of profits as well as by the weakening of their authority as employers. At the same time, in this structure time alternating between delay and advance is accomplished through a precipitous rhythm; it is closely linked to an erratic time characteristic of economic crises, difficulties and conflicts resulting from the politics of colonial expansions and the propensity towards imperialistic wars. Thus alternating time and erratic time are united against the time pushing forward with which they compete strongly for its first place, and partially succeed in supplanting it. The first place in this time scale, therefore, is occupied jointly by the time pushing forward and by alternating time as well as by erratic time. These three times do not succeed in arranging themselves in an hierarchy and, thus, are in persistent conflict.

The second place in this hierarchy is occupied by the explosive time of creation. This is manifested in general strikes, in the early experience of the seizure of power by the proletariat, as for example, the Paris Commune, in the proletariat's expectation for social revolution, in the great technological inventions, the automobile, the airplane, the use of electric power in industry, radio and electronics.

In third place is the deceptive time of large administrative organizations of the political, labor and the military realms. This time is also manifested in the activity of trusts and cartels, in their nascent efforts to plan economy for private interests. It covers up a merciless struggle between the time in advance and delayed time.

The retarded time and the time slowed down and of long duration occupy the last place in this scale; cyclical time is forced into the background almost entirely. The retarded time and that of long duration emerge in traditional circles, as well as in the midst of the classes in decline; they are often centered in the rural areas rather than in the cities and are prevalent only in the industrially underdeveloped countries.

Therefore, the time scale of the liberal democratic global structure of competitive capitalism could be sketched as follows:

(1) The time leaping forward challenged by the alternating time and erratic time would be on the first rung.

(2) Explosive time would come next.

(3) Deceptive time would take third place. Here, advance is hidden under delay, and delay under advance.

(4) The retarded time and the time of long duration being equal in importance would take the last place, while cyclical time would be pushed into the background.

Is there a significant divergency between the structure and the total social phenomenon in this type of society and thus are there two time scales? This divergency and double scale of time does not seem to appear in this type of society. The tumultuous forces in the total social phenomenon penetrate directly into the structure; the time scale of the proletarian class tends to advance in comparison to that of the global structure, and the time scale of the bourgeois class tends to delay more and more in relation to it, but both limit each other in the total social phenomenon. Evidently, this holds true only until the moment when this structure either is transformed into that of organized capitalism or else breaks down because of a social revolution or in a fascist *coup d'état*.

The awareness of the time scale in this type of structure and society increasingly eludes the State and is concentrated in the social classes and their organizations for struggle, namely political parties, labor unions or employer associations. The perception and conceptualization of time are ideological and political on the one hand, while linked to technology on the other.

But this political and technical orientation of the consciousness of time does not lead to *mastering it*. The society of liberal democratic type is characterized by the absence of centers which succeed in mastering the time of the global structure. Certainly, the bourgeoisie and the proletariat, the political parties and the labor unions and finally, the State, show certain tendencies towards mastering the social time scale, but all fail to achieve it. They are "carried by the time", independent of their beliefs, be it "progress towards well-being through free enterprise", or the "great day of the social revolution" which is supposed to solve all problems. The structures which follow in the society of this type are not always those awaited or desired.

THE TIME SCALES OF CONTEMPORARY SOCIETIES

We shall end this analysis with four types of global societies and structures which are in conflict today: the managerial society of organized and fully developed capitalism, the fascist techno-bureaucratic global society, the planned society organized according to the principles of the Centralized Collectivistic State, and the planned society organized according to the principles of pluralistic decentralized collectivism. Of these types of society, only those of organized capitalism and State-planned collectivism exist at this moment. Examples of fascist societies were Germany and Italy between the two World Wars, and even now in Spain and Egypt. The planned society of a decentralized type formed according to the principles of pluralistic collectivism, has as yet never been completely realized. However, certain precursory signs can be observed in a popular democracy such as that of Jugoslavia, in the efforts of planification by the labor government in Scandinavia and to a certain extent, by the after-war labor government of Great Britain after the second World War.

THE TIME SCALES OF THE MANAGERIAL SOCIETY OF
ORGANIZED CAPITALISM

This is the type of society which has acquired its greatest prominence in the U.S.A. and to some degree in Germany before and after Nazism, as well as in France now. But tendencies towards this type of society can be detected in many countries where capitalism has achieved prominence, or has been introduced into the country from outside. The economy is no longer left to free competition; it is planned in the private interest of trusts, cartels and corporations with the aid of the State which puts its vast bureaucratic machinery at the disposition of the employers.

We can characterize the structure of this type of society according to our usual criteria: (a) The State is at least partially in the service of private planning agencies who tend to dominate over all other groupings and to corrupt them by every means, (b) The passive masses predominate strongly, forcing back the community we-nesses; the last when they are active, remain around planning organizations, and when they are passive back local groups. (c) Organizations for economic domination are more accentuated than all other depth levels of social reality. The technological and economic patterns as well as the political and advertising slogans are diffused with particularly perfected techniques and fall into step with organization. (d) The beginnings of automation reduces the technical division of labor; this has repercussions also for a redistribution of social division of labor.

(e) Technical knowledge heads all social control. It dominates education and teaching, which are penetrated by political conformism. Morality, scattered among the various classes and social strata, as well as law and religion come last as means of social control. (f) The "technical civilization" dominates not only cultural works but human relations as well, making the instrument triumph over the act.

The time scale belonging to this structure is very tormented and also contradictory. Planning for the profit of the trusts and cartels appeals both to the time of creation and the time lagging behind. Deceptive time must be added in the vast organizations. The techno-bureaucratic groupings constituted and promoted in organized capitalism, integrated as they are with the bourgeoisie, penetrate the directing of the huge industries, the upper echelons of the state administration, the upper ranks of modern armies, as well as the directing of most of the political parties. This leads back to the time alternating between advance and delay which is hidden under the time in advance; in fact, it is only a kind of shadow trailing the automatic movement of machines. This ambiguous time is often linked with the middle classes revived by the new techniques and tossed about between the different time scales. The working class is both besieged and seduced by "technical civilization" and the "illusions of prosperity" and of well-being. Frequently it is betrayed by the bureaucrats of its own organizations. In spite of its tendency towards a time pushing forward and a creative time this class is caught up often in erratic time. Thus, this latter time is raised to a place of importance in the time scale of the global structure. Added to this, there is a decline in social mobility. For increasingly numerous strata within the classes, the passage from level to level becomes more and more difficult. This proliferation of strata more or less stabilized within a class accentuates time held back on itself and leads

143

to the reappearance and increased intensity of the time of slowed down, long duration.

It is extremely difficult to formulate the time scale corresponding to the structure of organized capitalism, much more difficult than identifying the time scale of the liberal democratic structure of competitive capitalism. In spite of this we can try to present the following outline. Alternating time, time pushing forward, deceptive time, explosive time of creation and time lagging behind compete with each other. Erratic time, which in the last analysis has the best chance of triumphing, is often linked with the time lagging behind. Cyclical time and time of slowed down long duration, although occupying the last place, are far from being annihilated. Cyclical time is manifested in the burdensome economic crises, and time of long duration is present in the administration of the State, in the direction of labor unions and political parties, and also in the economic strata.

The awareness of time is concentrated in the great bureaucratic machinery which becomes even more ideological and political and much more dependent on technology than in the liberal democratic regimes. The knowledge of the time is mechanized here much more easily, as the structure of organized capitalism is not inspired at all by any ideal of the future.

These same organized machineries – centers of knowledge of time – try to dominate and master the time scale but they only achieve superficial success in this for they are slaves to the machines which they produce and they are "sorcerer's apprentices" in relation to them. This is especially clear in organizations of economic planning.

The structure of this society tends once more to be detached from the subjacent total social phenomenon. The total social phenomenon time scale, in spite of its chaotic character, favors time leaping forward and explosive time more than does the superposed structure's scale. This situation may be an indication of the probable short duration of the structures of organized capitalism, menaced as they are by explosions or attracted by fascisms of different kinds.

THE TIME SCALES OF THE FASCIST SOCIETY
BASED ON TECHNO-BUREAUCRACY

Only recently has this type of society come into existence. The military victory of the allies, their policy after the war, the fall of Peron in Argentina, have not eliminated or averted the tendency towards societies of this type, a tendency which is today stronger than ever.

The structure of the fascist society consists of the complete fusion of organized capitalism with the totalitarian state led by the techno-bureaucratic groups arising from the trusts and cartels, banks, high administrative personnel and the specialized career military men.[1] The semi-charismatic leader who crowns this edifice is only a straw man for these groups which enslave all strata and classes of the population, and dissolve all free associations. The techno-bureaucratic groupings found their support in planned economy, conceived for their own profit, which puts at their disposal some extremely powerful, technical means. The chauvinistic and racial mythology, the slogan of "reestablishment of order" and the faith in national independence, abundance, "public salvation" or "harmony" are only screens behind which is hidden the techno-bureaucratic authoritarianism.

There are numerous parallels between this structure and that of organized capitalism; therefore we shall not analyze it according to our usual criteria. Nevertheless, they differ. The fascist society combines the totalitarian State with a kind of mystical or mythological delirium, cynicism and super-organization. This structure differs from organized capitalism in the following ways: its communion we-nesses are based on hatred and ecstasy which is artificially provoked and aroused by declaring war on every grouping which is outside the government organization; by a pronounced forcing back of law and morality to the last rung of social control, substituting in their stead an artificial stimulation of mythology expressed in the form of military and athletic parades. Education is transformed into a form analogous to the training of animals.

What is the time scale of this structure? The Totalitarian State makes a desperate effort for unification accompanied by economic and military planning which is stalemated in the end. This is because the structure fails to absorb or express the subjacent total phenomenon, and also because the different techno-bureaucratic groupings in power live in mutually con-

---

[1] Cf. our studies 'La technocratie est-elle l'effet inévitable de l'industrialisation?' in *Industrialisation et technocratie*, Paris, 1948, pp. 179–211 and 'Les oeuvres de civilisation et les structures sociales sont-elles menacées par le déchaînement actuel des techniques?' in *Structures sociales et démocratie économique*, Brussels, 1961, pp. 269–280, reproduced and modified in *La vocation actuelle de la sociologie*, Vol. II, 2nd ed., 1963, pp. 431–461.

tradictory times. The times which concern managers, directors of industrial trusts, high administrative personnel, career military officers and the "organization men" of the exclusive dominant party are contradictory. The outline for the time scale of this structure could be tentatively formulated as follows:

(1) Deceptive time and erratic time are raised to first place; deceptive time hides a time held back rather than a time pushing forward.

(2) It is followed very closely by cyclical time, a dance on one spot, which the fascists leaders take for the explosive time of creation. They were obviously mistaken.

(3) The time alternating between advance and delay related to the pre-eminence of the machine and technical processes takes over third place.

(4) The time lagging behind is fourth.

(5) The time pushing forward and explosive time are here only myths and illusions, or even hallucinations.

(6) The time of slowed down long duration takes refuge in all collectivities which resist integration into this structure.

In the total social phenomenon the times are chaotic but much nearer those of advance and explosion than in the structure.

The awareness of time is attributed to the fascist leader, to his entourage and to the leaders of the single dominant party. But this is an imaginary and illusory perception of time. Actually, they are blind to the effective social times. When the awareness of time is concretely manifested, there are definite conflicts between different techno-bureaucratic groupings which intertwine differently.

The same thing is true for the mastery of time. Certainly, the fascists regimes pretended to be able to master the time scale in which they moved, but in reality they were entirely enslaved by it. They found themselves even much more than the directors of the trusts in the situation of the "sorcerer's apprentice". The forces that they unleashed were extremely violent. Combined with the illusions which blinded them, these societies are literally carried along by the time in which they moves.

THE TIME SCALES OF THE PLANNED, CENTRALIZED, COLLECTIVIST STATE

Soviet Russia since 1917, China since 1949, most of the popular democracies, with the exception of Jugoslavia since 1950, illustrates this type of society.The capitalist enterprises and the bourgeois class are eliminated. The "absolutism of private profit", and "industrial feudalism" have disappeared. The proletarian class either alone, or united with the peasant class, is officially proclaimed "dictator". Nevertheless, this dictatorship is not exercised by the proletariat itself, but by the Communist Party which becomes the supreme organ of the State. It is charged with controlling the complete planning and collectivization of the economy, the execution of these plans, the "party line" and the "ideological line". Even though the industrial techno-bureaucracy, administrative, military and planning functions have become very powerful, they are tightly controlled. There is new proof of this in the recent measures calling for the local decentralization of the planning organizations. This control is in the hands of the State and its supreme organ, the Communist Party, which itself is in the hands of the organizer technicians. Neither the organs of planning, nor the techno-bureaucracy directing production, nor the State, nor the Party are directly controlled by the proletarians themselves. Freedom and actual or effective democracy in the economic, political and cultural realism, are only promised for the "second phase of communism, when the State will have disappeared". But on the XXIInd Congress of the Communist Party of the USSR the movement toward democratization and "self-government of masses" made real progress. In 1963 the introduction of self-government of workers in factories was officially promised by Khrushchov.

To characterize this structure according to our criteria: (a) The single party dominates over the State; the State is placed over all the other groupings and classes (proletariat, peasant, techno-bureaucrat classes, and middle classes). (b) Masses, sometimes active and sometimes passive, are accentuated in the global society; some active communions exist in the party, some active community-we-nesses in the Kolkhoses. (c) The depth level of social reality involving centralized planning dominates not only the economy, but the creation of new men and all the systems of symbols and ideas. Next comes the organized superstructure called on to implement this centralized planning, to represent the working classes and peasants, to direct the State, etc... (d) The technical and social divisions of labor are increased and combined with that of centralized planning. (e) In social controls, political knowledge has first place, technical and scientific knowledge comes next; humanistic education, a morality of ideal symbolic images and creation follow; and finally, art and jural regulations come last. (f) This civilization tries to synthesize humanism and technology, but thus far, without clear success.

What is the time scale corresponding to this social structure? All the organizations are directly affected by the global plans and are subordinated to the ideas, values and ideals which inspire the planifications. Only as a catalyst of spontaneous collective creation, can the organized superstructure realize effectively its extensive tasks and accomplish its purposes in the interest of all. That would presuppose the predominance of explosive time of creation and of time pushing forward which corresponds to innovating, reforming, effervescent behavior. But for these times to triumph it would be necessary that the interested themselves control the organizations. It is essential that the plans are not imposed from above and that they are not be dominated by the techno-bureaucrats of the single controlling party, or by the planners acting according to their own views, or by industrial managers commanding the workers in an authoritarian way. It would be necessary also that the city time and rural time are not in persistent conflict. As these conditions till now are not realized in the structure of centralized collectivism, the explosive time of creation is thence, limited by competing times, menacing its position at the top of the corresponding scale. Thus the outline for the time scale of this structure would approximately be the following one:

(1) The explosive time of creation and time pushing forward are challenged by the deceptive time of the vast organized superstructure not yet sufficiently controlled by the interested. These times are threatened also by the time alternating between advance and delay arising from the struggle between different techno-bureaucratic groups of party organizers, planners, managers, technical specialists and lastly from the passive resistance of the rural areas.

(2) Erratic time is characteristic of the dissatisfied, anxious, and oppressed working class.

(3) Time lagging behind and time of slowed down long duration continue to play an active role in the mores, as well as at the ecological and demographic base. Even in the symbolic spheres, this time is far more important than could be expected.

The time scale produced by centralized collectivism causes the structure to live in perpetual tension. In fact, this structure evolves on a taut line and it is perpetually menaced by fatigue, disillusion, and indifference on the part of the majority of its beneficiaries. Their reactions can lead to some surprises. Only a rapid transformation in the sense of the "self-government of the workers", as it is promised now could make this time scale less tense.

Therefore, as in all contemporary structures, the time scale of this regime clearly diverges from that characterizing the subjacent total social phenomenon. As to which of these two time scales favors explosive time of creation remains rather an enigma. Perhaps the interpenetration of the both time scales would be the best solution.

As to the awareness of time, the enormous organized super-structure of the single party pretends to be the only center able to grasp and know the social time scale. They do not recognize that mere mortals, whether united or not into groups and classes, might have this ability. This awareness of time is, furthermore, essentially pragmatic and indeed ideological. It is identified here with a practical goal: the effort to master the time scale of society of this type. One must recognize that this effort succeeds up to a large point, but the duration of this mastery remains problematic. More than this, time pushing forward and explosive time are to a large extent sacrificed to the deceptive time of the organized super-structure.

THE TIME SCALES OF THE PLANNED, DECENTRALIZED, PLURALISTIC COLLECTIVISTIC SOCIETY

This type of society has not as yet been completely attempted. Nevertheless, it is not an arbitrary construction but systematizes some real, observable tendencies. These can be seen as already mentioned in certain popular democracies as Jugoslavia, for example, and in certain Western Countries when they attempt collectivistic economic planning on a democratic base. Other examples are the Scandinavian countries and England at some periods. We will not discuss here the question of whether the movement towards a society of this type involves a social revolution, or whether it is the next step after centralized collectivism, etc. The structure of this global society would be founded on an attempt to establish a balance between industrial democracy and political democracy. The economy would be planned from top to bottom in a decentralized manner. It would commence with the workers councils of control and management of every factory and enterprise, passing on to the local councils of industry and the regional economic councils, ending in a central economic council of planification. There would be *federal ownership of the means of production* which would belong at the same time to all the councils mentioned, beginning with the councils of management of a factory and thence on to the central economic council. All the workers involved and consumers would participate in the ownership, individually and in groups. The State, itself decentralized, would be balanced by this independent economic organization controlled directly by all participants and *vice-versa*. A judicial body would resolve all conflicts between this federal economic organization and the State.[1]

To summarize the traits of such a global structure according to our criteria; (a) A multiplicity of equivalent hierarchies of economic groupings, on the one hand, and of local groupings, on the other, would lead to a global economic organization and to the political State, the two limiting each other reciprocally. (b) A predominance of the active *Community and communion* we-nesses. (c) Among the depth levels accentuated would be planning based on free consent, ideas and creative values; innovating and unforeseen social roles; open and diverse federated organizations. These levels, it is true, are challenged by patterns, and rules, especially by autonomous jural regulation. There is a powerful limitation of the technical divisions of labor by a developed automation, while the social division of labor is reinforced. (e) Knowledge is freed from ideology and gives a choice place to knowledge of *Others*, of the we-nesses and of groups. Law in its different forms plays an equally important role. These regulations occupy the first place in the hierarchy of social controls. Morality, particularly creative morality, morality of virtues and imperative morality come next, followed closely by education and art. (f) A new civilization is elaborated, preoccupied with giving to man and groups every means to dominate effectively the techniques and the instruments.

What would be the time scale of such a global structure? Here the explosive time of creation and time pushing forward appear to have an

[1] Cf. our descriptive essay in *The Declaration of Social Rights*, New York, 1945 and Paris, 1946.

effective chance to occupy first place. Nevertheless, the creations and the initiatives of different groups might easily be contradictory and conflicting. In fact, the interested, whether groups or individuals, could conceive their own interests very poorly and be opposed to innovations. In that case time alternating between advance and delay and even the time lagging behind would be next. Time lagging behind would be reinforced by the inevitable pre-eminence of law regulation in this structure which favors parity and equivalence among a large plurality of groups. Jural regulations always tend to lag behind. On the other hand, there is no longer any perceptible divergency between the structure and its subjacent total social phenomenon and this can push time behind as much as time ahead.

Awareness of time in this society would probably have as many manifestations as there are equally important groupings in balance. The mastery of the time scale would only be realized through an agreement by the principal organizations. This would not be an easy task to achieve.

CONCLUSION

In concluding this book we note again that it is not the task of sociology to evaluate the different time scales. Creative time and the time pushing forward can serve evil as well as good. This is equally true of time lagging behind. On the other hand, each social time scale, whether or not it is viewed as a means of realizing hierarchies of values, always presents some strong points and some weak ones, some advantages and some intrinsic disadvantages.

All that we wish to emphasize here is the great multipliticity of social times, their many possible combinations, and the time scales they form in relation to global societies of different types. An historian, M. F. Braudel, has recently accused me of wanting to enclose social times in the "skin of a goat", as Aeolus did with the winds, and to release these times to characterize particular social frameworks. I do not believe this accusation is justified. Each social framework, for me, produces its own times and often its own scale of times. I have never denied that the times can form varied scales and that according to the variations of the scales, the diverse social times interpenetrate one another and are unified in a particular way. But how can these interpenetrations and the unifications of these times corresponding to concrete collectivities be studied without first establishing a difference between them and following their complex dialectics? And for this task sociology, with its discontinuistic typological method, is better placed than history which always searches for continuities. But history utilizing sociological analysis of the plurality of time scales has more opportunity to show their variable, specific, and non-repeatable unifications. Thus both sciences must collaborate[1] in the study of the multiplicity of social time scales and their flow and ebb of unifications.

[1] See in Chapter II of this book the section on 'Sociological Time and Historical Time' (p. 34) and the already quoted paragraph of my *Dialectique et sociologie*, Paris, 1962.